# Off the Dusty Bookcase

Aubrey G. Stephens

Two-Gun Phoenix Publishing

OFF THE DUSTY BOOKCASE
A Two-Gun Phoenix Publishing Publication

All rights reserved under U.S. and International copyright law. This book is licensed only for the private use of the purchaser. It may not be copied, scanned, digitally reproduced or printed for resale. It may not be uploaded on shareware or free sites, or used in any other manner without the express written permission of the author and publisher. Thank you for respecting the product and work of all involved in providing this work to you.

OFF THE DUSTY BOOKCASE Copyright © 2025 by Aubrey G. Stephens
 by Aubrey G. Stephens
Editing by Sorella Smith
Cover Art by Shawn Howe
Book Formatting and Cover Formatting by Cookie Morris
Book Layout © 2016 BookDesignTemplates.com
Two Gun Phoenix logo by Percival Constantine

Two-Gun Phoenix Publishing
8892 Yorktown
Southaven, MS 38671

[twogunphoenix@gmail.com](twogunphoenix@gmail.com)

Publisher's Note: This is a work of fiction. Names, characters, places, and incidents are a product of the author's imagination. Locales and public names are sometimes used for atmospheric purposes. Any resemblance to actual people, living or dead, or to businesses, companies, events, institutions, or locales is completely coincidental.

Off the Dusty Bookcase / Aubrey G. Stephens. -- 1st ed.
ISBN 978-1-971151-06-9

**Putamus ergo Legimus!**

**Dedicated to Rick Jones-my best friend and fellow adventurer for 75 years.
I miss you, brother.**

# CONTENTS

The Old Library ............................................................................. 1
The Year When Stardust Fell ...................................................... 5
The Dracula Tape .......................................................................... 7
The Complete Compleat Enchanter ........................................... 9
The Mystery of Dr. Fu-Manchu .................................................. 13
The Prisoner of Zenda et al. ....................................................... 17
The Mad King by Edgar Rice Burroughs ................................. 19
Double Star .................................................................................. 23
Royal Flash .................................................................................. 27
Zenda Movies .............................................................................. 31
Russell Thorndike ....................................................................... 35
Edward John Moreton Drax Plunkett Lord Dunsany ............ 39
Manly Wade Wellman ................................................................ 41
Forgotten Juveniles Part I: Robert A. Heinlein ....................... 43
Forgotten Juveniles Part II: Paul French .................................. 47
Forgotten Juveniles Part III: Carey Rockwell .......................... 49
Forgotten Juveniles Part IV: Victor Appleton ......................... 53
Forgotten Juveniles Part V: Frank W. Dixon and Caroline Keene
  ........................................................................................................ 57
Forgotten Juveniles Part VI: Percy Keese Fitzhugh ............... 61
Forgotten Juveniles Part VII: The Cowboys ............................ 63
Three Interesting Stories ............................................................ 67
H. Rider Haggard ........................................................................ 71
She and Allan .............................................................................. 71
The Epic of Gilgamesh ............................................................... 73
Background for M.A.D. .............................................................. 75
Red Alert ...................................................................................... 79
Fail-Safe ....................................................................................... 81
Trinity's Child ............................................................................. 85
Alas Babylon ............................................................................... 87
On the Beach ............................................................................... 89
One Second After ....................................................................... 91
Night of Camp David ................................................................. 93
Seven Days in May ..................................................................... 95
Dr. Strangelove: or How I Learned to Stop Worrying and Love
the Bomb ...................................................................................... 97
The Dollar Series ........................................................................ 99
The Time Machine Stories from *Boys' Life* ............................ 101
Harry Bates and Don A. Stuart ................................................ 105
H. Beam Piper ............................................................................ 107

| | |
|---|---|
| Medal of Honor | 111 |
| Kelly Freas | 113 |
| The Space Willies | 115 |
| Last Man Off Wake Island | 117 |
| If the Universe is Teeming with Aliens ... Where is Everybody | 121 |
| The Writers of Star Trek | 123 |
| The Greenwich Village Hippies Trilogy | 127 |
| Theodore Roosevelt | 131 |
| Time For Rhyme | 133 |
| The TV Books Part I | 139 |
| The TV Books Part II | 143 |
| The TV Shows Part III | 147 |
| Doomsday Plus 1 | 151 |
| Shall We Sit and Talk a Little Treason | 163 |
| In Congress, July 4, 1776 | 167 |
| Constitution of the United States | 173 |
| Author Biography | 197 |

# The Old Library

**A reintroduction, review, and possible rant about forgotten, classic, authors, and oddities from across the range of genre types.**

I grew up in Meridian, Mississippi, the second largest city in the state at that time. Located near the city hall is a two-story Victorian building built in the 1880s. The city of Meridian bought the building in 1913. I had the great fortune to spend many hours wandering the nooks and corners of the fine old place.

You could easily picture it as a home of a wealthy family in the Victorian Age and even imagine an elegantly dressed stranger from Transylvania stepping through the double doors of the front entrance, or Holmes rushing up the hard wood stairs to the second floor, with a cry of "Watson, the game is afoot!" Turning left at the top of those stairs, you might see David Star and Tom Corbett staring out the window at the evening sky. In the far corner sits Tom Swift doodling on a sketch pad. Pay no attention to an emerald green curtain in the other corner.

Let's head back down the stairs ... why look there, in the room to the right I believe I see Woodrow Wilson Smith and across the hall Theodore Roosevelt preparing for his trip to Africa and isn't that Sir Richard Burton giving him tips for the trip.

Ok I'll stop now.

When the city bought the building, it became the public library. I did meet all the people real and fictional mentioned above in that building as well as hundreds of more and there were really all kinds of odd nooks in the different rooms. In 1968 it closed its doors and the city opened a bigger, newer, brighter library. I miss it, as the library. The building is still there. Not long after it closed as the library it reopened as the Meridian Art Museum in the early seventies. I got to attend the opening night soirée as well as the stage performance to raise money for the museum which confirmed, at least for me, that the building was haunted for there looking straight at me were Charles Dexter Ward, Fortunato Luchresi, Robur, Omar Khayyam, and Cardinal Richelieu. No, I didn't see an old stack of books. The art critic and performer who did the one-man show was Mr. Vincent Price.

I did spend some time in the new library in 1968 and 69 and have visited it since but it just wasn't the same. The smell of the books and the wood shelves and floors was missing. There are brightly lit bookshelves running in long lines, but no little nook where you could stumble on and find treasure and think to yourself where the hell did these come from?

Which brings me to the real reason for this; there was a day and time you could walk in a bookstore and find gems of writing from years before you were born. Granted in some genres there was far less being published than there is today but what was published tended to stay in print longer. But in the last twenty to thirty years authors that were well known during their lifetimes and for decades after have disappeared from bookstores and even worse from the knowledge of readers.

My feeling about this is a great disappointment for the readers who are missing so many great stories. Each time a writer's story is no longer read, a piece of his or her soul disappears. I like believing that every time a baby laughs a fairy is born, if you clap loud enough Tinker Bell will survive and if you read a writer's story a spark remains of his being.

In each chapter of this work now before you, I'll grab one of those no longer in print or hard to find and possibly forgotten novels off that dusty bookcase to review and reintroduce to you good readers. Come with me. We are about to time travel decades into the past and visit with some of my old friends that I hope will become yours as well.

I still miss that library.

# The Year When Stardust Fell

Raymond Fisher Jones (15 November 1915 – 24 January 1994) was an American science fiction author. He is best known for his 1952 novel, *This Island Earth*. He wrote 13 books and over 70 short stories one of which was the basis of the television show *Tales of Tomorrow*.

*The Year When Stardust Fell* tells the story of Ken Maddox and Mayfield, Colorado, the small college town where he lives. It's an American every town, a normal quiet little place where nothing out of the usual happens until the coming of the comet. The new comet that sweeps through the solar system and in the process crosses the path of the orbit of Earth so that the comet's tail engulfs the planet. Not a problem there you say, the Earth has been in the tail of comets numerous times over the centuries. Except this time the tail has a colloid in it composed of an unknown element.

The unknown element has the property of easily forming an affinity with metals so that the metal pieces in moving contact with each other very quickly form a cold weld and no longer move. Within days of Earth passing into the tail of the comets, engines, ball bearing, and other metal moving parts that modern society depends on cease to work. With the Earth due to remain in the tail for the next four months, nothing with metal parts will be moving.

Just in case you didn't know it, if the many trucks, ships, and other forms of transporting goods ceased to work any large, medium, or small city is three days away from starvation. So, what do desperate people do to feed themselves? The movement of mobs from the cities flows across the countryside. Sorry for this one before I use it ……...And winter is coming.

Having set the background of the book let me say that it is one of the Winston Science Fiction juvenile series released through the 1950s and 1960s. As other writers of the time period such as Robert A. Heinlein and Andre Norton who also wrote "juveniles," Jones does not treat his subject or his reader as juvenile. While you will not find naked blondes and cursing, *The Year When Stardust*

*Fell* is a well-crafted story with nicely developed characters and a sound basis in the science of the time that holds up well even fifty plus years later. This could have been a typical post-apocalyptic story but instead we are treated to a story of science and superstition. A well-crafted work understanding that the savage is just below the surface of the well-dressed Man in the suit and the shaman waiting to explain that we have pissed off the gods instead of looking for a logical, thinking reason.

With the clock set back to the Middle Ages can Ken and the college professors find a solution to the dust? Will the people of the town revert to following the ravings of Granny Wicks, the half-crazy old witch-woman or reach for knowledge? Can Mayfield last through the onslaught of the raiders and the approaching Colorado winter?

Considering that this novel was written in the heyday of the 1950s and for what we now call young adults it does step out of the good guy vs. bad guy and black and white no shades of grey world into one where there are a multitude of colors except the crimson of blood. It is an enjoyable read that at times makes the reader think.

So, gentle reader, with these few thoughts I leave you to blow off the dust, open the book, and step into a year with stardust falling. What's that you say? The book has not been in print in over forty-five years? Not to worry. I wouldn't do that to you. Luck is with you as it has fallen into public domain and you can easily download a copy from Project Gutenberg. Enjoy!

# The Dracula Tape

As you no doubt have deduced from the title, this one is a vampire story. So you my good readers will know, vampires do not sparkle nor do they give piggyback rides. I really haven't cared for the most recent incarnations of the undead. I much prefer the children of the night to mooning, whining, dithering vampires and their lovers.

*The Dracula Tape* is a 1975 novel that well may be the first time the vampire is the likeable protagonist of the story. In it Fred Saberhagan tells Dracula's side of the story in the Count's own words. It begins with a descendant of Jonathan and Mina Harker who stops one snowy night to pick-up a hitchhiker and the rider then proceeds to tell his version of the events while preserving it on a tape recorder. If it seems familiar, Saberhagan's book was published a year before *Interview with a Vampire*.

Bram Stoker's novel forms the plot of the story as seen from the Count's eyes. It fills in several holes that are in the original novel very well for me. Even when I read Stoker's story as a teenager I wondered why the heroes of his novel so easily bested Dracula. If we are to believe van Helsing, Dracula is a creature of great power and with hordes of animals and even control of the weather to aid him. The Count barely put up a fight in Stoker's tale. So, there must have been a motive behind his phlegmatic actions and behavior toward the group attempting to destroy him.

To Saberhagan's credit he gives us a Dracula who is charming, clever, and darkly humorous. His Dracula is an excellent storyteller. Stoker gives correlations between the fictional Dracula and Vlad Tepes such as his fighting the Turks plus his physical description of Dracula in the novel is very similar to the traditional image of Vlad Tepes. Saberhagan lets us know that his hero is Vlad Tepes - Vlad III, Prince of Wallachia – the Romanian hero that fought the tide of the Turkish invasion and, even though vastly outnumbered, stopped it from flooding the rest of Europe. He reveals to us the early year of Vlad's life and gives a solid background as to why Dracula is Dracula. He becomes a figure both terrifying and seductive. When he reveals to us the reason Vlad has no fear and his will to survive, we understand and accept him, even if we still feel a little uneasy around him.

I have always loved books you could sink your teeth into (Yep, I went there) and this one fits that bill. While Stoker's novel drags often, Saberhagen has a fast-paced story that urges you to continue reading well into the night. He, like Stoker, uses the more traditional aspects of the vampire – no turning to dust from the sunlight (it is uncomfortable but Vlad walks the streets of London with only minor effects.) Silver bullets – save them for the werewolves. If you are only familiar with vampires through the movies, a large number of the things used against them and powers they have are largely celluloid creations. Look not for them in the old legends.

*The Dracula Tape* is immensely enjoyable. Even if you find the story familiar from others picking up the ideas from it you can still look forward to an evening of good reading. The added plus to the book is finding that the story continues in six more novels. I have for a long time thought it a shame that Rice's Interview hit with the public and not this book. But then again would you really want to see Tom Cruise playing Dracula? A brief side note-when the movie *Bram Stoker's Dracula* was filmed, they asked Fred Saberhagen to do the novelization.

I leave you with a quote: "Children of the night, what music they make."

# The Complete Compleat Enchanter

The Complete Compleat Enchanter by L. Sprague de Camp and Fletcher Pratt is actually not just one work. You're getting five for the price of one.

Way back in the golden age of science fiction and fantasy the great editor John Campbell, after making *Astounding Science Fiction* the leader in the science fiction magazine field (as well as the best paying), launched *Unknown* as a companion to it. *Unknown* would run from 1939 to 1943. Campbell wanted stories to have a flair and humor that was lacking in tales featured in the then pulp top runner *Weird Tales*. With the first issue he achieved his goal with H. L. Gold's "Trouble with Water". It was a solid story about a New Yorker who meets a water gnome. The humorous fantasy and other stories in that issue would set the mark of quality that would continue for the magazine's entire run.

The May 1940 issue of *Unknown* hit the newsstands holding within its pages a jewel of a tale by L. Sprague de Camp and Fletcher Pratt, "The Roaring Trumpet" which would be the initial story in their Harold Shea series. De Camp and Pratt would co-author another four adventures in the series. The Harold Shea stories would run from 1940 until 1954 and only stopped then due to the untimely death of Fletcher Pratt.

Why you ask are they referred to as the Harold Shea stories? Harold Shea is the brash young psychologist that starts the train of events that leads him and his friends Reed Chalmer and Walter Bayard on their journey to adventure and love. In the "The Roaring Trumpet" we are introduced to the players and concepts that start all the fun.

Shea is out of place with the world or at least he thinks so. He drifts from hobby to hobby in a futile attempt to find the one which will complete his longing for daring do and the girl of his dreams. In the story, he arrives at work dressed in riding breeches and boots plus everything the horseman needs. His two colleagues bring out the point that he's off on a quest for adventure again. This brings them to another discussion of Harold's hobbies and how he is a bit of a misfit. Shea agrees with them and the conversation veers off to maybe there's a way to seek the worlds that his hobbies indicate he's looking to find. Reed speculates that parallel earths can be reached by employing a system of symbolic logic recodes the user's basic assumptions. Shea tells him to keep working on the idea and leaves to return the next day. Back Shea comes back dressed like a costume shop's idea of Errol Flynn as Robin Hood and carrying his fencing epee through his belt.

Reed gives him the formula he has worked out. Shea reads it and with a whoosh disappears. He finds himself in a world of snow, cold and desolation. He falls in with an old one-eyed man travelling toward the dimly seen horizon. Harold after a few mishaps finds his trip has ended and he has arrived at what looks like a farm located at the end of the world. After being introduced to the old man, Odinn, and hearing that he's looking to meet some guys named Thor and Loki Shea realizes that he's in the world of Norse myths. Even worse it's the time of the Fimburwinter and the approach of Ragnarök is not far away. Shea joins Odinn and company to help their mission and keep Ragnarök from happening and along the way maybe find a way home.

That's enough of a teaser for the story. There are more adventures waiting for Shea end his friends. In "The Mathematics of Magic", Shea and Reed find themselves in Edmund Spenser's *The Faerie Queene*. More hijinx follow carrying them to the next story. In "The Castle of Iron" after a brief stop in Samuel Taylor Coleridge's *Kubla Khan* our heroes find themselves plopped down in Ludovico Ariosto's *"Orlando Furioso"* for more fun and more problems. The fourth story has the bold adventurers landing in the "Kalevala" in the story "The Wall of Serpents". In *The Green Magician* our boys venture into their sixth world and the fifth novel of the Harold Shea series finding the world of Irish myth.

De Camp and Pratt create fun universes. They are well written and highly entertaining. The only problem I ever had with them was there aren't enough and when I first read them, they were difficult to find. But then came *The Complete Compleat*

*Enchanter*, all five under the same cover. There is one small hanging thread - What happened to Walter Bayard? But fear not good reader. De Camp returned to write more Shea stories partnering with several younger authors to do so and Walter's fate is ultimately revealed in a later story, "Sir Harold and the Gnome King."

Speaking of the later stories, while rereading the book I discovered that there are at least three that I missed and that Harry Turtledove has a collection of Shea stories I've never seen. So we shall end this chapter here as I'm off to read new Shea stories.

# The Mystery of Dr. Fu-Manchu

If you have never heard of Sax Rohmer, it is highly likely that you know the name of his most famous creation, Dr. Fu Manchu. Like Sherlock Homes, Tarzan, The Shadow or Dracula Rohmer's evil doctor gained entry to the lexicon of fictional people that have dropped into the pool of common knowledge. In this rare case, we have a villain who is more famous that the hero that fights him.

Ah yes, the hero of the book, Denis Nayland Smith or perhaps I should say Sir Denis Nayland Smith since he is knighted later in the series. Shockingly enough he owes his knighthood to Fu Manchu. Smith's constant struggle against him puts him in the spotlight, added to his saving the British Empire from Fu Manchu on numerous occasions.

*The Mystery of Dr. Fu-Manchu* is the first book and the first time Smith foils his nefarious scheme. Sherlock Holmes has his Watson, so too does Smith have his loyal friend to follow him to the edge of hell. Dr. John Petrie, a physician, so of course he is conversant with medicine, general science and-surprise-an expert marksman.

*The Insidious Dr. Fu-Manchu* isn't really a novel. It's actually a collection of short stories, thus the book lacks much depth and development. It could, however, be a textbook for a class on how to write a pulp novel. Each story contains a couple of brief chapters about the sinister Doctor. The constant action pulses forward as Smith and Petrie turn the tables on Fu Manchu by ensnaring him in his own devilish deadly trap. And then…and then… seemingly at the last second Fu-Manchu narrowly escapes. But we know he will be back.

Dr. Fu-Manchu is the incarnation of living evil, a maestro of assassination, a brilliant doctor, a dedicated connoisseur of torture, and an adept of the darker arts. A name that flows "trippingly on the tongue," he is a being that appeals and repels at the same time, and one can understand why his name became synonymous with evil.

> "Imagine a person, tall, lean and feline, high-shouldered, with a brow like Shakespeare and a face like Satan, ... one giant intellect, with all the resources of science past and present ... Imagine that awful being, and you have a mental picture of Dr. Fu-Manchu, the yellow peril incarnate in one man."
> — *The Insidious Dr. Fu-Manchu*

The novel was made into a Republic serial. Following that, Hollywood didn't fail to grab it with both hands. At least fourteen Fu Manchu movies have been made and one TV series. Overall, the first Fu Manchu novel is a fun read and makes one want to read the rest in the series. Some readers may have a problem with the "Yellow Peril" elements found in the books, but do be aware Sax Rohmer was writing these over one hundred years ago and he wrote to his time.

Here's a list of the novels written by Rohmer:

*The Mystery of Dr. Fu-Manchu* (1913) (US Title: *The Insidious Dr. Fu-Manchu*).
*The Return of Dr. Fu-Manchu* (1916) (UK Title: *The Devil Doctor*)
*The Hand of Fu-Manchu* (1917) (UK Title: *The Si-Fan Mysteries*)
*Daughter of Fu Manchu* (1931)
*The Mask of Fu Manchu* (1932)
*The Bride of Fu Manchu* (1933) (original US Title: *Fu Manchu's Bride*)
*The Trail of Fu Manchu* (1934)
*President Fu Manchu* (1936)
*The Drums of Fu Manchu* (1939)
*The Island of Fu Manchu* (1941)
*Shadow of Fu Manchu* (1948)
*Re-Enter Fu Manchu* (1957) (UK Title: *Re-Enter Dr. Fu Manchu*)
*Emperor Fu Manchu* (1959) - Rohmer's last novel.

I'll end with a couple of short notes of interest on Rohmer. He was a friend of Harry Houdini. Also, he died in 1959, due to an outbreak of influenza then known as the "Asian Flu".

# The Prisoner of Zenda et al.

The dusty tomes pulled from the bookcase for review this time around are *The Prisoner of Zenda* by Anthony Hope, *The Mad King* by Edgar Rice Burroughs, *Double Star* by Robert Heinlein, and *Royal Flash* by George MacDonald Fraser, as well as a possible mention of several other authors in passing and maybe a couple of movies.

Why four novels this time……read on.

The *Prisoner of Zenda*…. intrigue, sword fighting, gun play, damsel in distress, mistaken identity, romance and more. The beginnings of the story in short follow:

Rudolf Rassendyll, an Englishman of leisure, decides to avoid his sister-in-law's pushing a job on him by taking a quick trip to Ruritania. The Rassendyll family has a connection with the country from a visit by a member of the Ruritanian royal family many years before. The outcome of the visit was a scandal involving Rudolf's great, great something grandmother. This results in Rudolf having red hair and the events that follow his arrival in Ruritania.

He reaches his destination two days before the new king is to be crowned. He notices many people are staring at him and thinks it odd but goes about his vacation plans. Deciding to hike through the forest, he blunders into Colonel Sapt and Fritz von Tarlenheim who soon inform him that he bears a striking resemblance to the king. After having some amusing words with then he is invited to meet the soon to be king. They have a pleasant dinner where the king imbibes a great deal. Unknown to them a servant has placed a drugged bottle of wine at the table.

The next morning Rudolf and the others wake to discover that the king has been kidnapped by the forces of his cousin Duke Michael in an attempt to prevent his being crowned and replace him as next in line. Colonel Sapt and Fritz von Tarlenheim soon talk Rudolph into impersonating the king long enough to rescue the real king. He agrees and in his newly assumed role he meets Princess Flavia. They fall in love without her knowing he isn't the real king. Thereby hangs the hook of the book. Will the king being held prisoner in Castle Zenda be saved, will true love win through, will Michael's evil plan work, and will Rupert of Hentzau, Michael's chief henchman and a loveable rogue, win the hand of a second lovely lady staying at Castle Zenda?

Will I drop spoilers to answer these questions? Nope, I hate spoilers. The book is too good of a read and story to miss. It's a dashing romance with truly memorable characters and a great plot. I first read *The Prisoner of Zenda* at age 12 and was delighted to imagine the adventure of the attempt to rescue the chained king in the Zenda dungeon. For the romantic at heart our English hero is the ultimate British gentleman caught in a situation and a dilemma of love that echo with those wonderful but terrible words……what might have been.

The novel does leave some threads hanging, such as whatever becomes of that scoundrel, Rupert. Fear not; you can pick up the sequel novel *Rupert of Hentzau,* often included in some editions. Anthony Hope ties up many loose ends very well in the sequel. He brings back several old friends from *Prisoner* and lets the reader enjoy their company in a further adventure almost as dashing as its forerunner and just as romantic.

I could drop a few hundred more words to dangle before you about *The Prisoner of Zenda* but here's your chance to grab a copy and read it before the rest of the books and other items listed at the beginning are discussed in later chapters. Three reasons to do that; if you haven't read Zenda you should; if you have read it reread it and recall the fun; and it will make the reviews to come much more interesting. Plus, you can get both *The Prisoner of Zenda* and *Rupert of Hentzau* in e-reader versions online for free

Wait what's that noise? It's Colonel Sapt and Fritz von Tarlenheim calling for the Ruritanian cavalry to mount and ride with them to Castle Zenda to save the King.

I must away….

# The Mad King by Edgar Rice Burroughs

Edgar Rice Burroughs a writer with a hero that became a household name. You know the one, a book series stretching from 1912 until 1965, the one with the comic strip that ran for twenty years, the radio show, the comic book that ran for 40 years under four publishers, two television shows, and I've lost count of the number of movies – Tarzan (the only other character with more movies about him is Dracula). Yet Ed Burroughs wasn't just a one hit wonder. His second best known hero is John Carter. He found time between writing about those two to create several more series as well as many single novels and numerous short stories.

This time though we are focusing on Barney Custer, the hero of *The Mad King*. In this, our first discussed homage to *The Prisoner of Zenda*, our hero is an American. So how do we get our lad to Europe for his adventure? Of course, his mother fled the country of Lutha and having just lost an election bet that requires him to make the choice of either wearing a green wastebasket bonnet trimmed with red roses for six months or a beard for twelve. It is this red beard and saving an attractive young woman from a runaway horse and certain death that tips off the adventure, for the mad King of Lutha has escaped after years of confinement.

> "The wanted poster on a tree near the rescue point is read to Custer by the lady:
> "Gray eyes, brown hair, and a full reddish-brown beard," she read. "No matter who you may be," she said, "you are safer off the highways of Lutha than on them until you can find and use a razor.""

That and the fact he bears a striking resemblance to the King makes for continued conversation. They talk and she comes to believe that he is the escaped King and wants to get him to safety.

Both Anthony Hope and Burroughs were gentlemen of the Victorian Age. Hope was English and born in 1863 and lived through the height of Victoria's Empire. Burroughs was born in 1875 and an American and influenced indirectly by the same Victorian empire. Perhaps the best indication of their difference falls in their writing styles.

Hope is a proper English gentleman, and his writing is that of such a man. His readers may have been a little scandalized by it but his characters are Victorian in speech and manor.

Burroughs comes through as the looser style of American writing yet has the virtues and morals of a gentleman of that era, His writing is an easier read for someone reading his novels over a century after they were written. Here is a brief section from *The Mad King* shortly after the rescue:

> "The effect of his words upon the girl were quite different from what he had expected. An American girl would have laughed, knowing that he but joked. This girl did not laugh. Instead, her face went white, and she clutched her bosom with her two hands. Her brown eyes peered searchingly into the face of the man.
>
> "Leopold!" she cried in a suppressed voice. "Oh, your majesty, thank God that you are free -- and sane!"
>
> Before he could prevent it, the girl had seized his hand and pressed it to her lips.
>
> Here was a pretty muddle! Barney Custer swore at himself inwardly for a boorish fool. What in the world had ever prompted him to speak those ridiculous words! And now how was he to unsay them without mortifying this beautiful girl who had just kissed his hand?
>
> She would never forgive that-he was sure of it.
>
> There was but one thing to do, however, and that was to make a clean breast of it. Somehow, he managed to stumble through his explanation of what had prompted him, and when he had finished, he saw that the girl was smiling indulgently at him.
>
> "It shall be Mr. Bernard Custer if you wish it so," she said, "but your majesty need fear nothing from Emma von der

Tann. Your secret is as safe with me as with yourself, as the name of Von der Tann must assure you."

She looked to see the expression of relief and pleasure that her father's name should have brought to the face of Leopold of Lutha, but when he gave no indication that he had ever before heard the name she sighed and looked puzzled.

"Perhaps," she thought, "he doubts me. Or can it be possible that, after all, his poor mind is gone?"

"I wish," said Barney in a tone of entreaty, "that you...""

This is just a small taste of Ed Burroughs' writing, and I warned you before that I don't do spoilers, so you'll just have to read the book which is easily found for free online. While you're at it, go on and read the Tarzan and John Carter books. In fact, go for the Carson of Venus series as well. In case you can't tell I feel readers should at least try his works, if only to discover the Tarzan of the books and the many ways he is more that the ape man in the trees. Besides, don't you want to know if Barney falls in love with the girl he saves or is there a beautiful princess waiting for him?

# Double Star

First, if you haven't read or heard of Robert A. Heinlein, I am sadly disappointed with the bookstores in your area and your fellow science fiction readers there as well for not introducing you to his works. Robert Heinlein was one of the writers discovered by the great editor John Campbell. Heinlein became one of the icons of the golden age of science fiction.

Now why is a science fiction novel falling into this multi-chapter discussion of *The Prisoner of Zenda*? Well, of course it's a retelling of the story. This time our hero is "The Great Lorenzo" as he bills himself or to those that know him, Lawrence Smith, a down-and-out actor. In truth, he is actually a superb actor. But alas no prince this time. and therein lays our story.

To kick off this space-based drama, the Great Lorenzo is approached for a job, to impersonate someone. Our hero tells the man trying to hire him that sort of work is below the dignity and status of a thespian of his fame. The hopeful employer then challenges Lawrence's ability to even attempt to double for another person and as he does gives him a makeup kit to use to show that he can, a kit that you might find on the aisle in a store at Halloween. The great actor scoffs at the kit, and the man turns away from him. Then, using simple items present, Lawrence changes his stance and facial expression and tells the chap to turn around.

"Where did he go?" are the first words out of his mouth. Lawrence has without really trying become a different man. Now the man speaking with him must have him for the job.

Why? The fate of the solar empire is at stake. The man Lawrence has to double for isn't just a simple movie star or singer that needs a double to use to dash out a back door to fool their fans. No, it's John Joseph Bonforte, the most well know politician in the solar system. He's been kidnapped. Without his guidance war looms between Earth and Mars. A few words for context here: *Double Star* was written when there was still a small possibility of intelligent life with a civilization on Mars and long before Ronald Regan became president.

Heinlein takes the hero, prisoner, and rescue plot line and makes it his in *Double Star*. He did it so well that the book won the Hugo for best novel in 1956. He also wrote a type of coming-of-age story and does a truly excellent job. In short, he creates a character that you like and want to see what happens to him and as he discovers what he is capable of.

If you haven't ever read Heinlein, *Double Star* is a fun place to start. I highly recommend you add Heinlein's work to your repertoire.

*Off the Dusty Bookcase* 25

# Royal Flash

This time we take a look at a great grandson of *The Prisoner of Zenda*. We'll have all of the following: a cad, a rogue, a scoundrel, a rake, a rascal, a blackguard and, surprise, our hero is all of those. May I introduce you to Col. Sir Harry Flashman V.C., KCB, KCIE, and sole survivor of the battle of Piper's Fort.

Harry Flashman is the creation of George MacDonald Fraser. Some of you may have run across the name of Harry Flashman from having to struggle through "classics" of English Literature, specifically *Tom Brown's School Days* by Thomas Hughes. In this story of an English public school Harry is the school bully. He's finally thrown out of the school for being brought back to the campus in a wheelbarrow stone cold drunk. He gets possibly two paragraphs of mention in the 1857 novel.

Flash forward 112 years to 1967 when Fraser takes Harry Flashman, the bully, and makes him the hero of *Flashman*, the first novel in the series. Fraser reveals that after leaving school his father purchased him a commission in the British army. We soon learn that Flashy does have three great talents: languages, riding skills, and, to borrow a term from *Blackadder*, the old rump-pumpy.

To borrow a quote from Heinlein, "Adventure is someone else catching hell a thousand miles away," Flashy is a devout coward and would gladly let anyone but him be "the someone" of the pervious quote. He managed to fall into situations that place him in an adventure despite his best to avoid them. In the first novel he only wishes to lounge around London wearing his pretty uniform, drinking and chasing women. So naturally he finds himself posted to India just in time to be sent to Piper's Fort. Before you can say, "Where's the nearest house of ill reput?," the fort is under siege from a native uprising. Poor Harry doesn't know whether to cry, scream, or just wet his trousers.

The front gate falls and Harry like an intelligent man runs in the opposite direction. Bad luck, old man; bullets flying around, cannon shot knocking holes in the walls, and the colors dropping of the flagpole. What can Harry do? He trips over the flag line clipping his head on something hard, knocking him loopy, and as he falls to the ground, he manages to get the flag wrapped around him. As the world fades to black he hears a bugle call.

The relief column arrives to find all the fort's defenders dead except for gallant Harry Flashman who lies wounded in an attempt to save the colors. Harry is nursed back to health and sent home to England. Shortly after arriving the Queen awards him the Victoria Cross. Thus does Harry become a hero and the darling of Victorian society.

All of this leads us to *Royal Flash*. Flashy is up to his usual tricks, visiting a brothel with an old friend when a sudden police raid occurs. Being no fool he soon finds his way out through a window and is then hotly pursued by the coppers. Gaining some distance, he finds a coach waiting and ducks into it. A lovely lady enters the coach shortly after that and decided to help him hide, but her male companion will have none of it and calls the authorities over. Words pass back and forth from the lady to the copper to the companion and vice-versa. This continues until the officer recognizes Flashy as the hero of Piper's fort and, hearing a slight accent in the voice of the lady's companion. tells him to shut up and leaves. The companion stands there fuming as the woman tells the coachman to drive on without him, telling Flashy that Otto was a bore anyway. In the space of five minutes Flashman has made a conquest of Lola Montez, one of the great beauties of her age and future mistress of the King Ludwig I of Bavaria, an enemy of Otto von Bismarck one of the future major political forces in Europe.

Years later Flashman finds himself in Munich where he is abducted by Bismarck's agents. It turns out that Flashy has a strong resemblance to a Prince that Bismarck needs to have a double take the place of for a few weeks. The prince is also scheduled to marry a lovely duchess and Flashman has to take his place for that too. Bismarck hints that it may be a permanent replacement with Flashy staying on as prince with a beautiful wife and a kingdom.

So here we are back to the general situation of *The Prisoner of*

*Zenda*, but knowing our boy Flashman will he keep the girl, the crown, and the kingdom? No spoilers here but do read on.

Fraser writes a tale well worth reading and, in the process, weaves some new twists into the old story. He is adept at making the world he writes feel extremely real. Part of this may come from the research he does into the Victorian world. All the Flashman books have annotations throughout the stories that show how he mixes real people into his fictional world. Fraser could have easily written several histories of the Victorian Age but instead he gave us that history in the adventures of Harry Flashman.

I highly recommend you grab one of the Flashman novels and give Flashy a chance to pull you into his world. After rereading *Royal Flash* recently, I find that I've got to reread at least one more of the novels. So good readers, I shall leave you here and shortly be drinking tea and reading my favorite - *Flashman in the Great Game*.

# Zenda Movies

I know, good reader, you may be wondering how this series of reviews on *The Prisoner of Zenda* and its clones and grandchildren can have even another installment when I've covered all the books listed. I feel like it's important to mention a few movies. Sometimes we read a book then see the movie made from it or we see a movie like it and then read the book. I'll be discussing the former happening.

Very often when we do go see a movie made from a book we find as least a little disappointment in the film, especially if we like the book. I'm going to cover the films made from all the books covered and will do it in reverse of the time frame of how the novels were written. This mainly because *Prisoner* has had many versions made of it so I'm saving them for last.

*Royal Flash* was made into a movie in 1975. It stars Malcolm McDowell as Flashman, Oliver Reed as Otto von Bismarck, and Britt Ekland as Duchess Irma. McDowell does a fair job in his role but I've always thought that Michael Caine was a much better fit for the role. Oliver Reed is excellent as Bismarck and Brit Ekland is lovely as the ice duchess. Lionel Jeffries has a small role and he is always a joy to watch. To sum up the film version is worth seeing but read the book first.

The next two novels, *Double Star* and *The Mad King*, are easy to cover. Sadly, neither has ever been filmed. Both would make good movies and with all the bad science fiction movies that have been made, *Double Star* would be a good choice for a studio to invest some time and cash into making.

This brings us to the original *Prisoner*. It has been filmed in English at least eight times. The first two versions on film I can't speak of as they were silent movies made in 1913 and 1915 and no known copies have survived. I have seen still shots from both and they don't provide enough insight to tell much about them.

The 1922 silent version stars Lewis Stone as Rudolf Rassendyll

/ King Rudolf and Ramon Novarro as Rupert of Hentzau. It is the novel but in this case a lot of the flavor of the novel and the humor is lost due to it being a silent film. It is worth seeing for Novarro, who became a screen idol in the early days of movies.

I'm skipping now to the latest versions. There is a 1988 animated version that you can skip – not very good animation or voice acting. The 1984 BBC miniseries is somewhat of a mystery since I haven't been able to find a copy and the actor may be well known to British audiences but not as much to an American audience.

1979 saw the release of a version starring Peter Sellers in the title role. As a rule, I like Sellers in most of his roles. While *Prisoner* does have humor in it, it is by no means a comedy and somebody decided to make it into one. Their logic for doing this has eluded me for over 35 years. Sellers was very capable in acting in serious roles and in *Dr. Strangelove* and *The Mouse That Roared* we saw him do multiple roles but, in this version, we get the Inspector Clouseau goes to Ruritania. The good parts; there's the gorgeous Elke Sommer as the Countess and once again we get to see Lionel Jeffries ably perform in the role of General Sapt. Outside of that it really does the novel an injustice.

In 1961 there was a TV version from The DuPont Show of the Month. Christopher Plummer is our Rudolf Rassendyll / King Rudolf, Inger Stevens as Princess Flavia, and Mark Lenard playing Detchard (that's just to get the interest of all the Star Trek original series fans.) I have seen this version but not since it aired in 1961 but I do recall it so I must have enjoyed watching. Otherwise it would be lost from my memory with many other shows from that era.

Stewart Granger and Deborah Kerr have a go at it in 1952. Granger is handsome and Kerr is beautiful. Plus, you get James Mason as Rupert with his great voice and accent. But the film is a frame for frame remake of the 1937 version.

> 1937, the golden age version of *Prisoner of Zenda*:
> with Ronald Colman - Major Rudolf Rassendyll / The Prisoner of Zenda,

Madeleine Carroll - Princess Flavia,
C. Aubrey Smith - Colonel Zapt,
Raymond Massey - Black Michael,
Mary Astor - Antoinette de Mauban,
David Niven - Fritz von Tarlenheim,
Douglas Fairbanks Jr.- Rupert of Hentzau; a perfect cast for the novel.

Sometimes a movie gets made and once you see it, no remake will ever come close to the magic of it. This is one of those movies. It's also one of those very few movies that are the book. This is at least the one case where you can read the book and watch the movie and fall in love with it as much as you did when reading it. Good reader, grab a copy of the book and read it, then grab a copy of this version of the movie and spend a long evening in the Victorian Age and live with the sense of adventure and the playing fields of Eton.

P. S. If anyone has a copy of either the BBC mini-series of *Prisoner* or The DuPont Show of the Month version please get in contact with me.

# Russell Thorndike

Russell Thorndike was a British author who wrote his most well-known works during the golden age of the 1930s and 1940s. I doubt there are a great number of younger readers that have ever heard of him, but they still may know him from his great protagonist. Just as Rafael Sabatini created the swashbuckling heroes Scaramouche and Captain Blood, Thorndyke created a hero that is their equal.

For those unfamiliar with Thorndyke or his creation, may I introduce you to the Reverend Doctor Christopher Syn, Vicar of Dymchurch-under-the-Wall. His adventures will run through the years 1754 to 1805. You may well ask how is a quiet vicar of a small English town placed in the spot of becoming a dashing, sword wielding, champion of the people of Dymchurch? Could it be that Doctor Syn wasn't always a poor cleric?

Why of course not. He was once known as Captain Clegg, the notorious pirate who thought he would settle down to a simple life accompanied by his old friend and shipmate Mr. Mipps. They do this in the year of 1775. As most of you know the American colonies are being taxed by the government of King George III during this year and the years preceding it. They were not alone in bearing the weight of the King's taxes; the poor farmers of the Dymchurch are under the same boot. To ease their problem, they have resorted to smuggling. Mr. Mipps soon falls in with them and this leads to the Vicar of Dymchurch coming to their aide and finally assuming the role of their leader. Not as the Reverend Doctor Christopher Syn, but as the Scarecrow.

Thorndyke would write seven novels about his brilliant scholar from Queen's College, Oxford, where he also was taught his skills of riding, fencing, and seamanship. The novels were published in the United States at the same time as they were in Britain. They went out of print by the end of the 1940s, making it difficult for the following generations to find them to read or even know the wonderful character of Doctor Syn existed.

The Scarecrow was saved from disappearing, however, by a little movie making company deciding to make a movie of one of them. The little company, headed a by a guy name Walt Disney who had read the books years earlier and intended to make a three-part series for use on the Wonderful World of Color. Unbeknownst to Disney, Hammer Films had also decided to make a new movie of the Doctor Syn character since there had been a film made in 1937. So, the race was on.

Hammer was known in the early sixties for their horror films. This was the tact Hammer took with their 1962 version getting it done quickly. They filmed in black and white and changed the name of the film to *Captain Clegg* to avoid possible legal problems with Disney. It was known as *Night Creatures* in the U. S. with actor Peter Cushing in the lead role. Peter Cushing is the best reason to watch the film. He fits the book description of Doctor Syn very well.

In 1963 the *Wonderful World of Color* ran its three-part version called *The Scarecrow of Romney Marsh* and at the same time released a theatrical version in Britain titling it *Dr. Syn: Alias the Scarecrow*. It stared Patrick McGoohan in the title role and is a vastly better production than Hammer's, filmed on location around the Romney Marsh area and using St Clement's Church in Old Romney as Doctor Syn's Dymchurch parish church.

Walt Disney in the opening to "The Scarecrow of Romney Marsh" pulls a copy of *Doctor Syn* off his office bookcase for use in the introduction and of course the credits listed Thorndyke as the author. *Alias the Scarecrow* was a hit and would be released several years later as a theatrical production. Side story – it came close to becoming a weekly series but by then Patrick McGoohan had had a hit in the BBC series *Danger Man* known in the U.S. release as *Secret Agent*—so alas it never happened.

On the good side, the film did lead to the release of the seven novels again. They were fairly easy to find for ten years or so and in several editions but have become somewhat scarce over the years. The novels have fallen into public domain one way or another, and most are on line for reading now. Here's a list of the

Doctor Syn novels in internal chronological order:

> *Doctor Syn on the High Seas* (1935)
> *Doctor Syn Returns* (1936)
> *Further Adventures of Doctor Syn* (1936)
> *Courageous Exploits of Doctor Syn* (1938)
> *Amazing Quest of Doctor Syn* (1939)
> *Shadow of Doctor Syn* (1944)
> *Doctor Syn: A Tale of the Romney Marsh* (1915)
> *The Slype* (1927)

As you may have noticed there are eight books in the list. The last book, *The Slype*, isn't a Doctor Syn book but the good cleric and Mr. Mipps have great influence on the novel even thought they were long dead by the time the events of the novel take place in 1923.

Dr. Syn also made an appearance in Alan Moore's *League of Extraordinary Gentlemen*.

The books are not only a fun read and swashbuckling adventures but well written stories and you get to see the character of Doctor Syn develop over the years.

# Edward John Moreton Drax Plunkett Lord Dunsany

I would guess that few of my good readers have ever heard the name Edward John Moreton Drax Plunkett or even the short version of Edward Plunkett. But it is possible several have read of and likely read the stories of Lord Dunsany. Edward Plunkett was the 18th Baron of Dunsany and his works were published under the pen name of Lord Dunsany. Lord Dunsany was Anglo-Irish writer. His title is the second-oldest title in the Irish peerage and he lived much of his life in what is likely Ireland's longest-inhabited house, Dunsany Castle near Tara.

He was an avid hunter and saw Africa as a hunter in the early years of the 20th century, at the time of the rise of the great white hunter. Dunsany was a crack shot at one time being the champion pistol shot of Ireland. His games were cricket and chess of which he was a quiet good player. He invented a chess variant called Dunsany's chess.

Why then are we interested in Lord Dunsany? The question is best answered by the title of his best-known work, *The King of Elflang's Daughter*. The time frame of his writing spans from 1909 to 2002 though the 2002 work was a work prepared for publishing in 1957 just before his death, but remained unpublished until 2002. His output contains a wide spread of genres from fantasy to mystery. During his life time his writing was well received by both the public and critics. His works were not as numerous as other writers but all are well crafted pleasures to read.

Dunsany's works were easily found through the 60s, 70s and 80s but sadly here disappeared from bookstore shelves. Hopefully we may see a revival of their being reprinted. At this time unless you are already a fan and willing to pay for a limited-edition volume running in most cases well about the fifty-dollar mark, you only hope is to run across the paperback copies form the previously mentioned decades, and those may run you a good multiple of the original price.

Why read Dunsany? First, he is fun to read and if you do decide that you like his works there's something for you to look forward to reading. There is an unpublished 1956 short story collection that was discovery in the 1990s when a curator, at Dunsany Castle, locating and organizing the author's manuscripts, typescripts and other materials. Second is for the influence he had on other author's writings.

To give you an idea here a short list of writers and film makers that named him as having an effect on their work. They are in no special order: J. R. R. Tolkien, Guillermo Del Toro, H. P. Lovecraft, Robert E. Howard, Clark Ashton Smith, Talbot Mundy, C. M. Kornbluth, Arthur C. Clarke, Manly Wade Wellman, Evangeline Walton, Jack Vance, Michael Moorcock, Peter S. Beagle, David Eddings, Gene Wolfe Fletcher Pratt, and Ursula K. Le Guin.

Here my suggestions for you to start reading Lord Dunsany:

> *The Travel Tales of Mr. Joseph Jorkens*
> *Jorkens Remembers Africa*
> *The Gods of Pegāna*
> *Time and the Gods*
> *At the Edge of the World*
> *Beyond the Fields We Know*
> *Gods, Ghosts Men and*
> *Over the Hills and Far Away*
> *The Ghosts of the Heaviside Layer, and Other Fantasms*

I hope you'll give Lord Dunsany a try if you can find a copy. Just as an interesting side note here, a piece of knowledge about him. Dunsany married a handsome woman, Lady Beatrice Child Villiers in 1904. Just as Robert Heinlein found a great love and help mate in Virginia Gerstenfeld Dunsany's lady would be an aide to him and managed his works after his death.

# Manly Wade Wellman

I have spent many weekends in the Ozarks. While there I had a chance to wander a couple of trails through the mountain forest. Drifting in the hollows and hills I was put in mind of the stories of John the Balladeer by Manly Wade Wellman.

Wellman lived for many years in North Carolina. He was a writer of note during his lifetime. While he wrote across a wide range of genres he is best known for his fantasy and horror stories set in the Appalachian Mountains, many of which appeared in the classic magazine *Weird Tales*. His father was stationed as a medical officer in Portuguese West Africa where Manly was born in the small village of Kamundongo. His family returned to the United States when he was still a young boy. He lived in several states over the next few years. After receiving his BA in English, he attended Columbia Law School.

Manly chose to be a writer instead of a lawyer and from his first sell in 1927 until well into the 1980s he would be a favorite among science fiction and fantasy fans. He hit his stride in the early 1940s selling both to the science fiction mags and fantasy plus crossing over into detective mags and comic books. The first issue of *Captain Marvel Adventures* comics was written by him. While serving later on active duty in WWII as a lieutenant before going to war he took over the writing of The Spirit for Will Eisner who was already on active duty. He also wrote the comic *Blackhawk*.

In 1946 he received his first major award for writing by beating out William Faulkner for the Ellery Queen Mystery Magazine Award. I understand that Faulkner was highly upset. The story that won was "A Star for a Warrior," a Native American detective tale. During this same period his novel *Rebel Boast* was nominated for the Pulitzer Prize. The novel is sub-titled "First at Bethel, Last at Appomattox" from which you will gather it is set during the War of the Rebellion and tells the story of five young men and their trials during the bloodiest of our country's wars. His interest in doing a novel set in that period may have stemmed for him being named after Lt. General Wade Hampton III. He would write a biography of Hampton, Giant in Gray. It is well worth seeking out and reading if you have an interest in the history of the War of Southern Independence.

Wellman would write many more Civil War stories through the 1950s and 60s.

His best-known hero was John, aka John the guitar picker, Silver John, and John the Balladeer. John is a wandering singer who carries a guitar strung with strings of pure silver. Wellman never reveals his last name to us, just referring to him as John or John the guitar picker. Wellman had an interest in the folk tales and songs of the Appalachians, and it was there he would set the stories of John. John would travel the mountains with his guitar and a copy of *The Long-Lost Friend*. John was a veteran of the Korean War and self-educated. An expert shot, John uses his songs, silver strings and personal courage to defeat the mystical evil and strange creatures he encounters in his wandering.

Wellman wrote for both radio and television over his career and many of his stories were adapted for those media. Perhaps the best of these adaptations is *Still Valley* adapted by Rod Serling for the original *Twilight Zone* from Wellman's story *The Valley Was Still*; I'll let Serling's opening narration give you an idea of the story:

> "The time is 1863, the place the state of Virginia. The event is a mass blood-letting known as the Civil War, a tragic moment in time when a nation was split into two fragments, each fragment deeming itself a nation. This is Joseph Paradine, Confederate cavalry, as he heads down toward a small town in the middle of a valley. But very shortly, Joseph Paradine will make contact with the enemy. He will also make contact with an outpost not found on a military map—an outpost called the Twilight Zone."

The episode shows how well a story can be adapted to another medium.

# Forgotten Juveniles Part I: Robert A. Heinlein

Welcome to part one of my take on books written aimed at a youthful audience, the juveniles (or as we call them today, young adult.).

Robert A. Heinlein is not a forgotten author but as we've seen from other chapters a great number of the golden and silver age science fiction authors are not found on bookstore shelves in any large number. I've noticed in the chain stores that if they are there it is just one or two of their works. While it is common to find Heinlein's better-known novels, most of his juveniles have dropped off the shelves. Even in the used bookstores and specialty book dealers the juveniles are increasingly hard to locate.

Why all the bother about a book dating back 70 years for the oldest and 58 years for the newest plus a follow up only 55 years old? The main reason is that they are simply good reads. The other reasons all relate to the overall effect they had and the quality of the writing as well as the fact that a reader can pick up a little science and survival skills.

Heinlein wrote twelve juveniles for Scribner's publishing house from 1947 to 1958. His thirteenth submitted novel would be rejected and end his yearly appearance in the kids section of the library. It would also end his writing of "juveniles". There a reason for the quotation marks around juveniles. Heinlein didn't write juveniles. He did stay in the boundaries that Scribner set for him that closely followed the social limits of the late 1940s and 50s, but these twelve books were not written so that they talked down to his audience nor treat them as if they were a group that didn't think.

There is no linking factor between the twelve books beyond that of man's push to reach the stars. However, a few of the books do seem to fall into the timeline of Heinlein's future history overview.

Here's a list of the books in publication order:

*Rocket Ship Galileo*, 1947
*Space Cadet*, 1948
*Red Planet*, 1949
*Farmer in the Sky*, 1950
*Between Planets*, 1951
*The Rolling Stones aka Space Family Stone*, 1952
*Starman Jones*, 1953
*The Star Beast*, 1954
*Tunnel in the Sky*, 1955
*Time for the Stars*, 1956
*Citizen of the Galaxy*, 1957
*Tenderfoot in Space* 1958 - published in 3 parts in *Boy's Life* May, June, July issues
*Have Space Suit—Will Travel*, 1958

As a general path to follow through Heinlein's juveniles, *Rocket Ship Galileo* through *The Rolling Stones* cover the time of the moon landing and exploring the solar system. *Starman Jones* to *Tunnel in the Sky* are the beginnings of interstellar travel. The last two books are set in the future where star travel is well established and common.

I'm not going to attempt to go into covering each book but will briefly touch on my top favorites, in order of publication.

*Red Planet* is a story of the Mars that was possible from what we knew at the time, so we have Martians and an atmosphere close to breathable. Jim Marlowe and Frank Sutton are teenagers who get into trouble at their boarding school because of Jim's pet, Willis the Bouncer, a form of Martian life. They discover a plot that threatens both their parents and the Martian colony. Their journey to save both forms the core of the novel. Just a side note; the Martians in the book are the same race as in Heinlein's Hugo winning novel *Stranger in a Strange Land*. It is also a story of freedom and rights.

With all the TV shows about survival on the air today it's odd that some producer hasn't picked up Tunnel in the Sky to make into a series. Rod Walker is a high school student who is taking an advanced survival class. The class's final exam is to drop the students on planet they know nothing about. They can take all the equipment that they can carry and have to survive for ten days after which they are recovered and have passed the course. Rod elects to carry two knives. Shortly after his drop there is a nova that disrupts the Earth's ability to retrieve the students. Now they must survive for an undetermined length of time with only their skills and the one hint they were given. "Watch out for stobor."

The May 1958 issue of *Boys' Life* featured part one of "Tenderfoot in Space." That issue was my first introduction to the writings of Robert A. Heinlein and it along with the April 1947 issue with "Nothing Ever Happens on the Moon" got a lot of scouts reading him. Of course, with just a taste we had to go find other Heinlein tales. Those of us with good librarians got pointed to the Heinlein juveniles on their shelves.

A brief sentence or two on the last Heinlein that was to be published as a juvenile may be of interest. The novel that Scribner didn't accept was *Starship Troopers*. If you are new to reading Heinlein this is one of the books you are still likely to find on the bookstore shelves. It is well worth reading.

Our last Heinlein book is *Podkayne of Mars*. Some critics put Podkayne under the juvenile list, but it was written in 1963 well after Heinlein had left Scribner. If you read the unabridged printing it definitely wasn't a novel that would have been accepted for juveniles in the 1950s.

# Forgotten Juveniles Part II: Paul French

While Isaac Asimov is a well-known name, Paul French is not, but the two are connected. Paul French, the author of *David Starr, Space Ranger*, is a pen name Asimov used at the beginning of the series.

The book was created by Asimov at the request of Doubleday & Co as a juvenile to be used as the basis of a television series. Asimov, fearing the TV show would be akin to the awful stuff – his opinion - coming out on TV at the time, he agreed to write the book under a pen name. Paul French was born to keep his reputation as a science writer of non-fiction protected.

The television series fell apart but the book did well and he would continue write David Starr book, who was known after the first book as Lucky Starr, six in total. There was a seventh book planned but it was dropped when Asimov decided to focus on his non-fiction books for the next few years. While he never returned to the Lucky Starr book fortunately, he did return to writing science fiction which was lucky for us.

I'll list the complete series for you here but will focus on the first book to discuss the writing quality and style.

Here is the complete list plus one almost:

> *David Starr, Space Ranger* (1952)
> *Lucky Starr and the Pirates of the Asteroids* (1953)
> *Lucky Starr and the Oceans of Venus* (1954)
> *Lucky Starr and the Big Sun of Mercury* (1956)
> *Lucky Starr and the Moons of Jupiter* (1957)
> *Lucky Starr and the Rings of Saturn* (1958)
> *Lucky Starr and the Snows of Pluto* (planned but never written)

As the reader can see, the novels were written in the decade of the 1950s and the science of the books was true to the concepts of the time. Asimov did write a preface for later editions that explained to the reader that the advance of scientific knowledge made some of the ideas out of date and simply wrong, like Venus being a cloud covered ocean planet.

David Starr as we learn in the first book lives in A.D. 7000. Mankind has covered the solar system and spread to the stars. David (named after Asimov's son) is a biophysicist well thought of by the Council of Science. The Council will play a larger part in the later books.

The novel is set on a Mars that is not too far removed from the Mars we know today. The atmosphere is one fifth that of Earth's and there are no canals but fissures are mentioned. which agrees with what is now known. This Mars has human settlers. David goes to Mars because several hundred people on Earth have died from eating foods grown on the red planet. He sets out to solve the mystery of why this is happening and in the process meets people that will return in later books of the series. He also receives the equipment that will allow David Starr to become a Space Ranger as well as gain the nick name of Lucky Starr.

Perhaps the best way to describe the books is to say that Lucky Starr the Space Ranger is a future embodiment of The Lone Ranger right down to the mask and faithful companion.

The books are fast paced action adventures, as well written as you would expect from Isaac Asimov. They are the only books that he wrote that take place in the solar system, his others are either on Earth or well out from our solar system. They are well worth tracking down for a fun, fast read and a look at another series that inspired some of the men that did put man on the moon and still reach for the stars.

# Forgotten Juveniles Part III: Carey Rockwell

The author discussed in this chapter…never existed. The books make up the series featuring Tom Corbett – Space Cadet. The writer of the series according to the covers of the books was Carey Rockwell. Carey Rockwell had no existence beyond being a house name for Grosset & Dunlap. There are eight books in the Tom Corbett series. Unfortunately, no records exist of who the authors were, but Willy Ley was the technical advisor to the series. I'll give Ley a small section after covering the Space Cadet books.

Joseph Greene was a comic book, science fiction magazine, radio, TV, and film writer in the nineteen forties and fifties. In the early fifties he was working for Grosset & Dunlap as an editor. Several years earlier he had thought of an idea for comic book story and submitted it, but it failed to be accepted. He reworked the idea as a radio script for a potential series as *Tom Ranger*. The radio series never panned out and in 1949 he recycled it once again into an idea for a newspaper strip called *Tom Ranger Space Cadet*. By that time Robert Heinlein had published his juvenile novel *Space Cadet*. Green contacted Heinlein and licensed the use of *Space Cadet*. The newspaper strip didn't come together and in October of 1949 it was renamed and became *Tom Corbett – Space Cadet* and rewritten as a TV series. The new script did sell to TV and was produced with the show premiering in October of 1950.

The TV series was a hit with kids and Grosset & Dunlap soon followed with the book series. It is thought that Heinlein's *Space Cadet* had a measure of influence on the books. While there aren't any known records of who wrote the books there is a general belief that Greene edited and plotted some of the books and possibly ghost wrote some of them if not all eight. He would write the Dell comic book series of Tom Corbett's adventures.

Tom was the hero of the book with two sidekicks following him closely. They and the world they live in are introduced to the reader in the first book *Tom Corbett – Space Cadet Standby for Mars*. The boys are very cookie cutter 1950s idealized teenage boys, this coming from the real-world ideas of how teenagers should be at the time the books were written and with the books being 1950s juveniles.

The first book starts in a fairly common way that the following books tend to stick to. The guys are at the Space Academy when they stumble into a grand adventure. Following them in the eight books we get the tour of the solar system along with the hint that interstellar travel may be coming. This never came into play since it's a big system and the popularity of the show waned in TV due to it shifting from network to network and the quality of the writing on the show degrading.

The science in the books is more pseudo-science than being based on solid knowledge of the day about the solar system and how things work. They do have more than enough action to go around and can be thought of as kiddie space opera. There is no romance though the boys do notice girls. And of course, no females in the Solar Guard. Can't have that; after all it is the 1950s, old boy.

The list of Tom Corbett books:

*Stand by for Mars* (1952)
*Danger in Deep Space* (1953)
*On the Trail of Space Pirates* (1953)
*Space Pioneers* (1954)
*Revolt on Venus* (1954)
*Treachery in Outer Space* (1955)
*Sabotage in Space* (1955)
*Robot Rocket* (1955)

In case you're a collector the last in the series seems to be the one most difficult to find. The rest pop up for sell fairly often.

Returning to the technical adviser for the series, Willie Ley was one of the early supporters of space exploration and travel. He was born in Germany and fled the country in 1935 after becoming disgusted with the rise of the Nazis. He would finally settle in the

United States. From then until his death, he would write dozens of non-fiction books on space travel. He would be known to several generations of young people from these books and his technical advice on many science fiction and non-fiction TV shows and films. Ley died on June 24$^{th}$ 1969 just over a month before the moon landing. Sometimes life is just damned unfair.

# Forgotten Juveniles Part IV: Victor Appleton

Victor Appleton, the listed author for the Tom Swift series, was a house name, a creation of Edward Stratemeyer in 1910. He wanted a young hero to capture the imagination of the kids of the new century like the Horatio Alger books of the last century had done with much success, financially and otherwise.

Tom would begin as a teenager with a mechanical-technological bend and a sense of adventure. The first book would have Tom tinkering with a motorcycle and this would continue for a while as he tinkered with or repaired an existing device. Later he would come closer to inventing by improving on current technology. Tom would go on for thirty-three volumes with Tom growing older and eventually marrying his best friend's sister. Sales of the books dropped with the marriage and stopped twelve volumes after that with the belief of the publisher that teenagers couldn't identify with an older married man.

But Tom Swift wasn't done. He would return a few years later written by Victor Appleton II. Same company same hero, he had just become Tom Swift Jr. Tom Jr. was more of an inventor than his father and would go on to bigger and better things than the original. Swift Jr. would be more suited to the atomic age as he picked up the family line in 1954.

I first ran across Tom Swift wandering down the shelves of my Junior High School library. I found still sitting on one shelf *Tom Swift and His Big Dirigible; or, Adventures Over the Forest of Fire*. It was originally written in 1930 and I'm reasonably sure it had been in the library from then until I found it and read it in 1962. I enjoyed it and went looking for more but alas there were none on the shelves --- Quick! To the public library, but no luck there. I had no recourse but the book section of hardbacks at the small city equivalent of a true bookstore. There to my pleasure I found the Tom Swift Jr. books and happily paid the enormous price of a dollar for my copy of *Tom Swift and His Triphibian Atomicar*. It was quickly read and shelved next to the treasured Tom Corbett books where it would remain for many years even though it would not be reread as many times as Tom Corbett. It remains in my library yet but now is shelved across the room for the Corbett books.

Tom Swift books would continue to be published on and off for the next thirty years with the last book being published in 2008. In whole there are 73 titles featuring Tom Swift or Tom Swift Jr., far too many for me to list here. I will list the first 10 of each series and wish you luck in finding them. The books are great to read and to share with your children or grandchildren.

Tom Swift Senior books:

*Tom Swift and His Motor Cycle; or, Fun and Adventure on the Road*, 1910

*Tom Swift and His Motor Boat; or, The Rivals of Lake Carlopa*, 1910

*Tom Swift and His Airship; or, The Stirring Cruise of the Red Cloud*, 1910

*Tom Swift and His Submarine Boat; or, Under the Ocean for Sunken Treasure*, 1910

*Tom Swift and His Electric Runabout; or, The Speediest Car on the Road*, 1910

*Tom Swift and His Wireless Message; or, The Castaways of Earthquake Island*, 1911

*Tom Swift Among the Diamond Makers; or, The Secret of Phantom Mountain*, 1911

*Tom Swift in the Caves of Ice; or, The Wreck of the Airship*, 1911

*Tom Swift and His Sky Racer; or, The Quickest Flight on Record*, 1911

*Tom Swift and His Electric Rifle; or, Daring Adventures on Elephant Island*, 1911

Tom Swift Jr. books:
*Tom Swift and his Flying Lab* 1954

*Tom Swift and His Jetmarine* 1954
*Tom Swift and His Rocket Ship* 1954
*Tom Swift and His Giant Robot* 1954
*Tom Swift and His Atomic Earth Blaster* 1954
*Tom Swift and His Outpost in Space* 1955
*Tom Swift and His Diving Seacopter* 1956
*Tom Swift in the Caves of Nuclear Fire* 1956
*Tom Swift on the Phantom Satellite* 1956
*Tom Swift and His Ultrasonic Cycloplane* 1957

# Forgotten Juveniles Part V: Frank W. Dixon and Caroline Keene

Frank W. Dixon and Caroline Keene, alas they don't exist. These were the author names used for the Hardy Boys and Nancy Drew book series, possibly the most successful of the juvenile books series we have seen so far in our review of forgotten books. The protagonists were young detectives; they would start in the 1930 and run for decades with one making a comeback with a reboot in 2010.

We'll go with ladies first. Nancy Drew is an attractive eighteen-year-old woman. She lives with her father in a small town. She is a role model, being an active, independent, well-educated young woman. She's out spoked and daring. For some unknown reason she keeps falling into mysteries. She solved them with her wit and courage, and it didn't hurt that she came from an apparently very well-off family since she never seemed to have trouble finding the funds to do as she wished. She would remain this way through the 1930s and 40s.

With the arrival of the 1950s Nancy would have a minor reboot to update her to the time period. There was a drawback to this. Nancy would lose some of that independence and free spirit to become the socially acceptable teenager of the fifties. Gone was the somewhat feminist young woman and in place we got the conformist. But luckily the curious would stay and the mysteries would continue to fall into her lap. Have no fear; Nancy still has grit and will win through.

This second incarnation of Nancy would survive the 1950s and 1960s, only to have a reboot in the 1970s. This attempt would not have the commercial success of her forerunners nor the fans. By the 1980s she was merely the shadow of the girl she once had been – a ghost haunting the libraries and used bookstores of the country.

Nancy Drew is a good series to relax with and have a quick mystery to read. The only drawback is finding the older books but stick with the books from the series' beginning through the 1960s. Beware that some may find them politically incorrect, just remember when they were written and don't judge the series from today's politically correct views.

Here's a list of the first ten books:

*The Secret of the Old Clock*
*The Hidden Staircase*
*The Bungalow Mystery*
*The Mystery at Lilac Inn*
*The Secret Of Shadow Ranch*
*The Secret of Red Gate Farm*
*The Clue in the Diary*
*Nancy's Mysterious Letter*
*The Sign of the Twisted Candles*
*The Password to Larkspur Lane*

The oldest still running juvenile book series features the Hardy Boys. Frank and Joe Hardy had their first adventure mystery way back in 1933, *The Tower Treasure*. Teenage boys loved the book and a series was born that would still have the boys solving crimes and mysteries eighty- nine years later. The ageless brothers are still a going concern. Like Nancy Drew the Hardy Boys would see change in the run of the series as well as a couple of reboots.

In the first incarnation, the boys would age slowly over the passing years until the fateful day one of them got married. This would set up the minor reboot of the boys in the late forties with the reasoning being teenage boys don't identify with older married men, even those that were only a few years older than the reader. The bottom line of company finances backed this thought up with declining sales of the Hardy Boys (Hardy men) series. The series returned Frank and Joe to their mystery solving ways, once again as teenagers in the 1960s.

This new reboot in the sixties would see the boys well into the seventies. There would even be a brief mingling of the Hardy Boys and Nancy Drew. It failed to achieve a large audience and soon the Boys wer to kick off another restart.

The last makeover has worked since the Hardy Boys are still a pair of sleuths for kids and teenagers to find on the bookshelves. Sadly, they seem to be missing that spark that the original books of the 1930s and 40s had.

If you get a chance to grab a Hardy Boys book in hardback from off an old dusty bookshelf, do so. Take your chance to meet Frank and Joe or to return to their small city. Buy the book, find a comfy chair, grab a soda, dim the light and take off with the boys to solve the mystery of the Sinister Man in the Black Coat (not a real book but I thought it would make a great Hardy Boys' title.)

Here's the list of the first ten books:

*The Tower Treasure*
*The House on the Cliff*
*The Secret of the Old Mill*
*The Missing Chums*
*Hunting for Hidden Gold*
*The Shore Road Mystery*
*The Secret of the Caves*
*The Mystery of Cabin Island*
*The Great Airport Mystery*
*What Happened at Midnight*

# Forgotten Juveniles Part VI: Percy Keese Fitzhugh

This chapter is for all my fellow scouts of all ages. Those who are my age will recall fondly some of the series I'll discuss but there may be one that escaped them and for the scouts that came after me, you are likely to have never ran across the series at all but should recognize one character that will be the main focus.

The Boy Scouts of America began in 1910. Shortly after that, books about the scouts started appearing and by 1911 a magazine for scouts called *Boys' Life* was in publication. In 1912 the Boy Scouts of America bought the magazine and it became the official magazine for the BSA. I mention it not because it is forgotten (it's still going strong along with the BSA) but because many golden age authors appeared in the magazine. Some of their stories would only be available in the *Boys' Life* issues, for example Robert A. Heinlein's story A *Tenderfoot in Space* (original entitled *Tenderfoot on Venus*) published in 1958 wouldn't appear again until 1992 in *Requiem*. Here's just a few of the others to appear in its pages: Isaac Asimov, Bertrand R. Brinley, Catherine Drinker Bowen, Ray Bradbury, Van Wyck Brooks, Arthur C. Clarke, J. Allan Dunn William Hillcourt, John Knowles, Arthur B. Reeve, Ernest Thompson Seton, and Isaac Bashevis Singer.

There were numerous books series. I will just mention a couple such as The Boy Scouts in, at, and on - insert a place, event, or happening and there likely was a scout book about it. The one series I will bring to your attention is Percy Keese Fitzhugh's novels. He would create the scouts of "Troop 1, Bridgeboro, NJ," a troop that would have scouts in it that would move on to their own series of novels, primarily Roy Blakely and Walter Harris.

This brings us to our main scout of interest and the series to find for reading. Walter Harris was a scout somewhere between 12 and 16, his age is never set in the books. The first thing you would note about him is that he was undersized for his age. This would give him the name that scouts would know him by for the next 102 years: Pee-Wee Harris. This is also the title for the book series about Pee-Wee and the adventures he gets into. One might substitute 'troubles' for 'adventures' because Pee-Wee would usually start the pebble rolling that caused the landslide but he was the good scout and always prepared. With compass, pocketknife and a small supply of food to fill the empty pit that is his stomach, he muddles through to come out ahead of the game.

A list of the books about Pee-Wee Harris:

*Pee-wee Harris*
*Pee-wee Harris on the Trail*
*Pee-wee Harris in Camp*
*Pee-wee Harris in Luck*
*Pee-wee Harris Adrift*
*Pee-wee Harris F.O.B. Bridgeboro*
*Pee-wee Harris: Fixer*
*Pee-wee Harris: As Good As His Word*
*Pee-wee Harris: Mayor for a Day*
*Pee-wee Harris and the Sunken Treasure*
*Pee-wee Harris on the Briny Deep*
*Pee-wee Harris in Darkest Africa*
*Pee-wee Harris Turns Detective*

Also, these two stories are known to exist:

"Pee-wee Harris Warrior Bold" (1930) - published as a serial in *Boys' Life* magazine and "Pee-Wee's Gold Brick" - an unpublished manuscript

Pee-Wee would eventually become a comic strip in *Boys' Life* in 1952 and the strip still runs today.

# Forgotten Juveniles Part VII: The Cowboys

Before we get into the biggest character in the cowboy juvenile market of the early Twentieth Century, I'd like to tip the white hat to a few honorable mentions: Hopalong Cassidy, Roy Rogers, and Gene Autry. The movies and TV shows featuring the three are aimed toward kids, just as the books about them were. All three would have several Big Little Books and would be featured in at least one of their own books.

Hopalong Cassidy was featured in a series, but he was very different from the character portrayed by William Boyd - smoking, drinking, and other unsavory habits. But here's

Whitman Publishing printed four Gene Autry novels in the late 1940s and one Roy Rogers novel in the 1950s. Whitman was the major Big Little Book publisher and they had a larger size replacement for them that was introduce in the late forties and ran until the late seventies. They were still undersized compared to a standard hardback book and didn't have the illustrations on every other page. Let's hum a bar or two of *Back in the Saddle Again* and *Happy Trails* to remember Roy and Gene then move on down the trail with…

A cloud of dust, a fiery horse and a cry of Fran Striker leads us to…that masked man.

Fran Striker is not a name that comes to mind for most people as the creator of an American icon. Yet in the 1930s he introduced not one but three heroes that would be a familiar name to the kids of nearly four decades and two that are still well known.

Striker's third best known hero started out appearing in the series *Challenge of the Yukon*, which changed to *Sergeant Preston of the Yukon*. The good Sergeant would last into the fifties and fade away shortly after.

For those that haven't figured it out, Striker's best known and longest lasting creation was the masked rider of the plains – The

Lone Ranger. First created for the radio in January 1933, he proved so popular that Striker was asked to turn his radio scripts into a novel. His schedule didn't allow it at the time so the first novel was written by Gaylord Dubois and as the cover page of the first book says, the novel was inspired by the radio series written by Fran Striker. Striker would later go back and re-edit and rewrite the first book so that in later editions the Gaylord Dubois credit was dropped. Striker wrote all the further novels and Big Little Books as well as some of the comic books and newspaper strip.

Striker would write nineteen novels about the Ranger with the last one appearing in 1956. He would also write thirteen Big Little Books with the last one published in 1950. Fran Striker died in an auto crash in 1960. There would be another Big Little Book done in the late sixties but it was not as well written as the Striker ones. After that it would take until 2012 for new Ranger stories to see book covers. There was a collection of short works *The Lone Ranger Chronicles* and a full-length novel *The Lone Ranger: Vendetta*, both from Moonstone Books. I have both on my to read shelf by my desk but have refrained from doing that until after writing this chapter. I wanted to just comment on the Striker books.

The Striker novels as a whole are a pleasure to read. He writes well and his stories move rapidly. His Ranger remains as he originally conceived the character through all his works. Luckily the books are easily found on eBay and many used bookstores with older books have them as well.

At the beginning of this book you're now reading, it says, "A reintroduction, review, and possible rant about forgotten classic authors," and I suppose I could claim that Striker falls under that since his creation clearly does not, but also note he is still listed on the title pages of the 2012 books as the creator. The reason for that sentence is I want to talk about the Ranger.

Ranger Reid is a member of a Texas Ranger posse that is ambushed and left for dead. Reid survives and is found by Tonto the Indian warrior who nurses him back to health. Tonto digs six graves and comments to Reid that he is now "lone ranger." Reid cuts a mask out of cloth, dons it and becomes "The Lone Ranger."

The Lone Ranger has been visually portrayed in a few different ways over the decades. The version that is burned in our collective psyche comes from the classic television series. It had more impact on the idea of the Ranger than any other element other than Striker's original concept and comes the closest to being the "ideal" Ranger.

Striker's idea of the Ranger met the perfect match in an actor in 1949 with the start of the TV series. There had been two movie serials before then but they didn't quite make the cut for portraying the Ranger. The actor that would step into the Ranger's boots was Clayton Moore. It was a match made in cowboy heaven. From the very first time until the last time Moore wore the Ranger outfit, he would never break character and never be seen without the mask. The Ranger's creed, a set of rules the Lone Ranger lived by, is a hard one to follow. Clayton Moore and fellow actor Jay Silverheels (Tonto) would do their best to live up to it.

In fact, Moore did it so well no one since he has had a chance as the Ranger. The last three attempts at bringing the Ranger back on the big screen and the little screen have all failed. I think the main reason is they haven't tried to do the Ranger as originally conceived. Instead, they have tried to do an updated Lone Ranger for whatever reason and it just doesn't work. I have hopes that someone will try again.

Here's the list of Lone Ranger books:

*The Lone Ranger* (1936)
*The Lone Ranger and the Mystery Ranch* (1938)
*The Lone Ranger and the Gold Robbery* (1939)
*The Lone Ranger and the Outlaw Stronghold* (1939)
*The Lone Ranger and Tonto* (1940)
*The Lone Ranger Rides* (1941)
*The Lone Ranger at the Haunted Gulch* (1941)
*The Lone Ranger Traps the Smugglers* (1941)
*The Lone Ranger Rides Again* (1943)
*The Lone Ranger Rides North* (1943)
*The Lone Ranger and the Silver Bullet* (1948)
*The Lone Ranger on Powderhorn Trail* (1949)
*The Lone Ranger in Wild Horse Canyon* (1950)
*The Lone Ranger West of Maverick Pass* (1951)

*The Lone Ranger on Gunsight Mesa* (1952)
*The Lone Ranger and the Bitter Spring Feud* (1953)
*The Lone Ranger and the Code of the West* (1954)
*The Lone Ranger and Trouble on the Santa Fe* (1955)
*The Lone Ranger on Red Butte Trail* (1956)

To close I'll mention the other hero that Striker created. May I introduce you to the grandnephew of the Lone Ranger......The Green Hornet.

The Hornet had several Big Little Books and a 1940s comic book series as well as a current one, a movie serial and a TV series. Yes, I know there was a Hornet movie a few years ago but I'm trying to forget it.

# Three Interesting Stories

The main problem with the three tales covered in this chapter is locating them. First of the three is the *Necronomicon* by Abdul Alhazred, followed by *The Grasshopper Lies Heavy* by Hawthorne Abendsen, and last but not least *The Sound of His Wings* by Robert A. Heinlein.

If you remember the first chapter of this book you now hold, you will recall that I spoke highly of the old public library in my hometown. It was a wonderful old building with many nooks and crannies that often led to finding treasures to read that were missed the last time I passed an area. It was in one of these cubbyholes that I found the *Necronomicon*.

It was a grimoire of strange and terrifying tales and hints of secret knowledge to be gained by its reading, a work composed of words snatched from the winds of the desert night by Abdul Alhazred, called "the Mad Arab" by many. Alas the afternoon I found it I was running late getting home from school and had forgotten my library card, so back on the shelf it went.

It was several days after I again returned but found it was on the restricted area for someone doing research, so once more I could not check it out. It remained forgotten until many years later when the library had moved to it new shiny building that I sought it out again, only to find it listed as missing from the shelves in the card catalog.

I've heard rumors that there is a copy at some university library in Massachusetts and one in the antiquities section in the Congressional library in Washington D.C. Someday....

Let us touch on Hawthorne Abendsen's *The Grasshopper Lies Heavy* for a few sentences. *Grasshopper* is a thrilling alternate history novel. Abendsen gives Harry Turtledove a run for the money as the best writer of alternate history. *Grasshopper* dives deep into a strange tale when the outcome of World War II is shifted toward the other side winning the war.

The world envisioned in *Grasshopper* is one of an ever-present cold war where the chance of tipping the world into Armageddon awaits the turn of a key. Great Britain bears little resemblance to the one we know and our own country is an alien place. While a terrifying vision of our world gone mad, *The Grasshopper Lies Heavy* overall remains a great read.

Finally, we come to Robert Heinlein's *The Sound of His Wings*, a story developed shortly after the heyday of Billy Sunday. One of Heinlein's future history stories, it tells of a preacher and his rise to political power. Designed to come just before *Logic of Empire* it fills us in on the background of how Nehemiah Scudder became a messianic figure just not for his church flock but for millions of people who felt politically disenfranchised. With "blood in the streets and blood at the polls but Scudder won the election. The next election was never held." In today's political world this is a story that is way too real in the reading.

I'll stop there. For my readers that by this time haven't figured it out I've been pulling your leg just a little. None of the above books and stories really exist. *The Necronomicon* is a pure imagination from the pen of H.P. Lovecraft. You can look all you wish but you'll never find it, though there are a couple of false copies around. One that pretends to be written in Arabic but is really nonsense and the other is a cover slapped on the writings of Aleister Crowley.

*The Grasshopper Lies Heavy* is a book within a book. It comes from the novel *The Man in the High Castle* by Philip K. Dick. All that I wrote about *Grasshopper* above is very true about *The Man in the High Castle*. It is a somewhat disturbing novel but an excellent read. Dick said he wrote it using the Y Ching, a Chinese fortune telling device that figures greatly in the real novel and the novel within it. It has been made into a TV series but do yourself a favor; read the book before catching the TV series.

*The Sound of His Wings* does appear in Heinlein's published timeline for his future history series, but he never wrote it when he first listed it in the 1940s and felt there was no reason to write it later on after other stories and novels had filled in the future history timeline.

I've wanted to read other novels and stories internal to other books or that were meant to be written but never happen to be written for many reasons. I just wanted to share these with you. I would read the last two with great enjoyment and the Necronomicon I'd seal in lead and then drop it into the deepest part of the Marianas Trench.

# H. Rider Haggard
# She and Allan

Sir Henry Rider Haggard (22 June 1856 – 14 May 1925) was an English writer most known for his pioneering the lost world genre. Most of his works are set in Africa and were written during the time that a good deal of the continent was still marked unknown on many maps. Haggard would create archetypal characters and places that are standard figures in our literature and movies today. The main two most readers would identify would be the ruminates or degraded remains of some ancient culture and the great white hunter.

His best known and easiest to find books are *She* and *King Solomon's Mines*. Both books have remained in print since their publication. She or Ayesha the beautiful goddess/sorceress and Allan Quartermain, hero of *King Solomon's Mines*, have been familiar characters for over 130 years. They and Haggard's writings have inspired many other writers. Those readers that are fans of Edgar Rice Burroughs will have no problem seeing the reflection of Ayesha in La of Opar from the Tarzan stories. Allan Quartermain is even more familiar with his being included in *The League of Extraordinary Gentlemen*.

For those that haven't read Haggard this may help you get an idea of his hero Allan Quartermain. If we were to take Indiana Jones and his quest for the lost ark to 1912/13 and turn the Germans into the Kaiser's men or the Czar's men making it a continuation of the great game, then turn it into a novel and publish it as a Haggard novel there would be no real questioning that Haggard hadn't wrote another adventure about Allan.

*She and Allan* brings together Haggard's two most popular characters. In a real world time line, *She and Allan* is published forty plus years after both King Solomon's Mines and She. In Haggard's internal time line King Solomon's Mines comes before

<u>She and Allan</u> and <u>She</u> falls after. All three are fully standalone novels so there is no need to read one before the other, though it is rather fun to read them in order

Haggard's writing style while that of a Victorian is still very readable. He also writes from personal knowledge for he lived in South Africa from 1875 until 1882. The picture he gives of the peoples he knew is a very sympathetic one. He admired the Zulus and saw them at the height of their power. When Great Britain annexed the Transvaal, Haggard was the government official that raised the Flag and read the announcement of the annexation. He was still there for the disaster of the British army at Isandlwana and the gallant defense of Rouke's Drift. (Side note-readers that don't recognize these names, go rent Zulu and Zulu Dawn or find the several excellent books on the Anglo-Zulu war. Zulu is about 85% historical correct and Zulu Dawn follows close to that as well.)

Haggard is a romancentic and his treatment of both Allan and She shows this influence in his life and the lives of his creations. As an illustration Haggard fell in love with a young lady; he courted her and sent her a marriage proposal; she returned it. He left for Africa and a government career to make his fortune. By the time he returned to England seven years later she had married (it is thought at the insistence of her family.) Haggard moved on with his life and married several years later. Many years after this the old love was put in contact with him. He discovered that her husband had abandoned her and her children. Haggard would see to their well-being until her death in 1907.

Good reader, go seek adventure with Allan long before Tarzan arrives in Africa and Henry Jones Jr. has found his first whip. I suspect you will be please to get to know Allan and friends and of course the most beautiful Ayesha – She Who Must Be Obeyed!

# The Epic of Gilgamesh

It is now time to discuss a one-of-a-kind fantasy/hero/myth adventure and the oldest story ever, so far anyway. Why the oldest you ask? *The Epic of Gilgamesh* is the oldest intact and complete writing that mankind still has to read. The epic dates back as far as 2500 B.C. While there are shards of other written pieces that date earlier there are no complete stories that are as old and most of what there is are fragments which bear nothing resembling a story.

The Gilgamesh story has influenced many of the ancient writings that have passed on to us from those times. It likely had influence on the works of Homer, even possibly the blind poet's actual words, if he existed, but surely on those who wrote his supposed epics down. It still speaks to us today as it did to those ancient Sumerians and Babylonians that sat to hear the adventures of Gilgamesh, the being that was two thirds god and one third man. They thrilled to hear how he set out to find fame and how he learned to master his own faults.

For the general reader the best way to describe Gilgamesh is his being a combination of Batman and Doc Savage. He has a deep dark side yet seeks to become more than he is at the start. Just as Doc and Batman acquire sidekicks so does Gilgamesh, though Gilgamesh gets his in a much odder way then they do. The gods decide to cause him problems and create Enkidu, a wild man that ravages the countryside. But what to do about this rampaging monster? The first step was for Shamhat, a sacred temple prostitute, to use her beauty to seduce the wild man. After enjoying her pleasures for seven days and seven nights Enkidu is rejected by the wild and goes to the city with her. Shortly after that he meets Gilgamesh and they fight. Gilgamesh wins the fight and they become lifelong friends.

As an interesting side note in the *Star Trek: The Next Generation* episode "Darmok" there is a reflection of the epic where Captain Picard is Gilgamesh and the alien Captain is

Enkidu. There is also a possible reflection in Philip Jose Farmer's novel *A Feast Unknown*. The two protagonists "Lord Grandrith" and "Doc Caliban" are thinly disguised versions of Doc Savage and Tarzan. In the novel the bronze godly man Doc Caliban fight several times against Lord Grandrith the Wildman but in the end they become allies if not friends against a greater evil.

Gilgamesh and Enkidu have adventures together and become as close as brothers. But their feats have made some of the gods angry so the gods decide to cause one of them to die. Enkidu is the one selected. After railing against his fate Enkidu dies. This sends Gilgamesh's life into a downward spiral. He leaves his city and sheds his fine garments to wear nothing but animal skins. He wanders the wild. While in his self-imposed exile, he hears of a man called Utnapishtim that lives on a far of mountain and who has the secret of immortality.

Gilgamesh determines to find Utnapishtim and get the secret from him. After traveling many days and a great distance he at last reaches the mountain and finally finds Utnapishtim. He demands to know how he became immortal. Utnapishtim tells Gilgamesh of how he learned that the gods were going to destroy mankind by a great flood. The god Ea decided to help save him and told him to build a boat and take his family and all the animals of the field aboard it. The storm that brings the flood lasts for seven days and seven nights and Utnapishtim and his family survive and their boat comes to rest on the mountain where Gilgamesh found him.

Enlil, the god who had sent the flood, arrives to find survivors and is extremely angry, but is confronted by the goddess Ishtar and the god Ea who berate him for his overreaching punishment. After hearing their words, Enlil blesses Utnapishtim and his wife and rewards them with eternal life. Gilgamesh discovers that immortality is a unique gift. His story doesn't end there but I have given enough spoilers.

*The Epic of Gilgamesh* is an epic poem like *The Iliad* and *The Odyssey* and just as you can find translations of both of them you can find many good translations of Gilgamesh's story. Do so and discover the fate of the world's first Hero – Gilgamesh.

# Background for M.A.D.

This chapter will serve as an introduction and background history for the next six books we'll be taking off the dusty bookcase. In short, it's all about M.A.D.

No, we aren't going to be covering issues of Mad Magazine. M.A.D. is an acronym for Mutual Assured Destruction. It is very likely that readers under the age of forty have not run across the acronym before unless they have read histories or seen documentaries of the cold war or science fiction from the time period dealing with World War III. M.A.D. was the philosophy the two superpowers in the world used to prevent nuclear war.

To give you a better understanding, let me tell you a fairy tale. Once upon a time there was a large family that lived in a nice house. And just as families do in stories this family had two uncles that lived in the basement of the house. One was named Sam and the other was named Ivan. Both men disliked the other and neither trusted the other. Both thought that if they failed to watch the other, he would be murdered in his sleep. So, they had divided the basement into equal halves and built a half wall between the sides. Thinking to defend themselves, they both bought giant black powder cannons. The cannons were loaded with double canisters (think giant shotgun shells.) They then surrounded the cannons with hundreds of pounds of black powder just in case they needed it, even though the firing of the cannons would have killed them and destroyed the basement with just the loads in them. Both men realized that to fire either cannon would kill both of them and totally destroy the house above them, yet neither would relent. Both would sit and stare 24 hours a day waiting for the other to move while holding the lanyard to fire the cannons in their ever more shaking hands.

Sam (the United States of America) and Ivan (the Union of Soviet Socialist Republics) would maintain this insane, oops, I mean M.A.D. policy for over forty years. How did we manage to refrain from slipping into a nuclear war if only by accident? Looking back now, a large part was played by pure damn luck. On at least ten occasions the world came within minutes and possibly seconds of a nuclear Armageddon.

Were the men that allowed this world killing Mexican standoff to exist insane? Many good writers of the time contemplated this question as well as what would happen if the M.A.D. policy failed. At the time men who thought that there was a better way or wanted to reduce the numbers of weapons were called crazy, traitors, or just unrealistic.

Why talk about these books today? After all, the U.S.S.R. ceased to exist twenty-five years ago. To all appearances, it seems the world is once more slipping into that all too familiar condition, apparently having failed to learn from the mistakes of history. We may unfortunately be about to repeat them. We came close at one point to ridding the world of nukes but alas we let the chance slip through our fingers.

Here's how the world stands as of late 2025:

Russia: Approximately 5,459 nuclear warheads.
United States: Approximately 5,177 nuclear warheads.
China: Around 600 nuclear warheads.
France: About 290 nuclear warheads.
United Kingdom: Approximately 225 nuclear warheads.
India: Between 150 and 160 nuclear warheads.
Pakistan: Between 165 and 170 nuclear warheads.
Israel: Estimated to possess around 90 nuclear warheads.
North Korea: Estimated to have between 30 and 40 nuclear warheads.

As you can easily see from the list above, there are still more than enough nukes to go around. If you have been watching the news in the past months, you know there's still plenty of people willing to throw bombs and some of them may not be sane.

The list of books to be covered on the subject are as follows:

<u>Alas Babylon</u>
<u>On the Beach</u>

<u>Red Alert</u>
<u>Fail Safe</u>
<u>Dr. Strangelove</u>
<u>Seven Days in May</u>
<u>Night of Camp David</u>

Happy thoughts and sweet dreams, good reader, if you can sleep after reading any of them.

# Red Alert

From 1958 until 1968 the Strategic Air Command of the U.S.A.F. maintained a 24-hour/365-days a year airborne wing of nuclear armed bombers on alert. They would fly a pattern from their base in the U.S. to a point close to the U.S.S.R. where they would go into a waiting pattern, then turn to begin their path back home to their base. As those planes were approaching home another group was on their route to approach the Soviet Union.

This was the height of the Cold War between the United States and the Union of Soviet Socialist Republics. Both countries had insane numbers of nuclear weapons aimed at each other. The Doomsday clock regularly passed the five-minute mark and it was a 70/30 bet maybe even 80/20 that the two would in the near future destroy each other in a rain of atomic fire and in the process take the rest of the world with them.

Peter Bryant was a pen name for Peter George. He wrote *Red Alert* while on active duty with the Royal Air Force. He had been a flight lieutenant and navigator during WWII and became a fighter controller in the 1950s. Much of the realism of the novel comes from his experience while serving. He wrote the book to show how easy it could be for a war to start and the dire results that could happen.

The novel itself concerns three groups: the crew of the bomber Alabama Angel, parts of the Strategic Air Command, and the President of the U.S. and his cabinet. It focuses on the strain of command and what can happen if one link in that chain snaps.

The General in command of the 843rd Bomb Wing flying the new B-52's is the link that fails. The pressure and strain of command combined with failing health causes him to decide to attack the Soviet Union using war plan "Wing Attack Plan R." This is a plan that gives a lower echelon commander the power to attack because under it all the higher command points have been reduced to a smoldering ruins and radioactive ash floating on the winds from a Soviet sneak attack, a' la "Pearl Harbor." The bomber crews have a recall code that only he knows. Each plane of the Wing is armed with two nuclear weapons. The general seals his base off from the rest of the world after sending the attack code. It helps at this point if you realize that the book was published in 1958 long before the internet, cable TV, and every home didn't have a TV.

North American Air Defense soon notices that the Wing is flying into Soviet air space and attempts to contact it and is ignored since the crews are trained to disregard any communications not using the correct code. The President is quickly informed. He and his advisors meet in a "safe" area and are now faced with the most critical decisions that they and the President will ever have to make.

For a novel written over sixty years ago, *Red Alert* still has the sitting on the edge of your seat feeling. It gives you a real sense of the actions and feelings of the bomber crew as well as putting you there with the President for the "What the hell do we do now" thoughts. All the action in the book takes place in two hours as you might have figured from the original British title. A quick reader can finish the novel in about the same length of time.

It may be over sixty years old but *Red Alert* is worth the time to find and read.

# Fail-Safe

Once again, we are in the time of the cold war. The U.S. and the U.S.S.R. are toe to toe in a nuclear standoff. It's October 1962. President John F. Kennedy and Soviet Premier Nikita Khrushchev are in a deadly duel over Soviet missiles and bombers in Cuba. The event that would be known as the Cuban Missile Crisis to history started on the sixteenth of October and lasted for thirteen days, finally ending on the twenty-eighth of October. This was the real world and in the middle of the crisis most people thought bombs would be dropping within days. It's the only time that U.S. forces have gone to Defcon 2. At Defcon 1 bomb and missiles would be falling.

Three days before the crisis started the Saturday Evening Post would publish a novel by Eugene Burdick and Harvey Wheeler entitled *Fail-Safe*. It would run in the magazine for the issues of October 13, 20, and 27 and be released as a hardback book in early 1963.

Fail safe is the point that Strategic Air Command bombers would fly to and hold at waiting for orders to either return home to their bases or to proceed to head into the airspace of Russia and attack. SAC crews were honed to a fine edge to do their mission and had the best equipment in the Air Force. SAC was the nuclear sword of the United States. The men were watched to ensure that they were stable from the lowest rank to the highest. The right code to release weapons had to be entered in a device. SAC assured Congress and the American public that nothing could go wrong go wrong go wrong.

In *Fail-Safe* we start the story by being introduced to a translator working at the White House, A General and a Colonel, a congressman and a businessman. All are doing their day-to-day jobs. The translator is reading articles in Russian magazines; the General and Colonel are giving the congressman and businessman a tour of the War room.

The tour is going well both men are impressed. The businessman expounds that his company builds a portion of the gleaming machines chattering around them. The General is pointing out the big board that shows the location of SAC aircraft and even Soviet submarines off the coast of the U.S. As he and the visitors turn to chat about the cost of all that they have seen, they are interrupted by an alarm. They look back to the big board and see a flashing light indicating an unidentified flying object has crossed into Canadian airspace on track heading for the United States.

More men enter the room and take up positions at consoles. Everyone's attention is focused on the flashing dot. Fighters are scrambled. Ground alert bomber crews rush to their planes and prepare to take off.

The General assures the two civilians that this happens several times a week and that the UFO is most like an airliner slightly off course. They watch the board and more information rolls in to inform them that the UFO is traveling at over 500 miles an hour. Suddenly the UFO drops off the board just as an attacking Soviet bomber might do to get below radar. The alert condition goes one step up. The ground alert bombers launch and more fighters head into the air. Minutes pass and nerves go taut and sweat forms in the small of the back. Then the blip is back. Canadian fighters have spotted it and made radio contact. It's a BOAC flight that lost power, then regained two engines. All is well.

Except one flight of six SAC bombers is continuing to fly past their fail-safe point. The recall message is resent. No response; they fly onward.

At this point the translator comes back into the story. He is escorted to a secret part of the White House and there he sees the President and his secretary. He joins them in an elevator that will take them to a command room far below ground. The President informs him he will be translating the words for both himself and the Russian Premier.

Unknown at that point a computer part has failed and the Russians are trying out a new jamming system both of which send the plane on their bombing mission and send the world to the edge of nuclear Armageddon.

*Fail-Safe* is a well written thriller that will leave you chewing your fingernails if you weren't too busy using your fingers to turn the pages of the book. It gives a good look into the world of what could have happened and almost did several times. An interesting quirk of the time is the fact that the authors felt easy actually using the real name of then Premier of the Soviet Union Nikita Khrushchev for their fictional Premier. Yet the President of the United States is never named but the descriptions of him make it easy to identify him as John Kennedy. The bombers in the novel are called Vindicators but from the information given and looking at the cover illustration of the magazine publication it is clear they are B-58 Hustlers, the first U.S. bomber capable of Mach 2 flight.

Written fifty-five years ago the book still holds up well. If you can use the term enjoyable about nuclear war it is an enjoyable book to read. It is likely to be found on the shelves of a good public library and easily found for sale. Read the book and then check out the movie version starring Henry Fonda.

# Trinity's Child

In this week's novel of slipping into nuclear war, we are moving up in our time period. From the 1960s we are traveling to the 1980s. To do so we need to bring our frame of reference up to date. Once more our protagonists will be a combination of the President, assorted military senior officers, and the crew of a B-52.

Our year is 1983. Ronald Regan is president; the Soviet Union is still a world super power. The Strategic Air Command is still the shining star of the Air Force. But the world has changed. No longer do the gleaming B-52s fly in the air on alert status going to their fail-safe points. That S.A.C. procedure had been dropped in 1968 with the reason given being to ensure more safety having had several crashes involving B-52s carrying nuclear weapons. The alert 52s now sit on ready pads by the runway on their bases. The alert crews can be no more than five minutes away from their planes and if the alarm sounds, the planes can be in the air within ten minutes and headed on their missions.

*Trinity's Child* uses the political situations of the world in the early eighties as a background for its setting. In the novel the Russian Premier faces the pressures of the United States upgrading its planes and missile systems and his military hounding him about the threat of a first strike from the United States. Because of this, he decides to commit to his own first strike. The command is given and the Russian missiles and submarines and planes begin the attack.

As the missiles and planes are in route the Premier uses the teletype hot line to message the American President telling him that it is a limited strike brought on by the United States' continuing aggressive policies against his country. He also states that there are three options that can now occur 1. The U.S. can take the hit and nothing more will happen, 2. The U.S. can retaliate with a like amount of force and the Soviet Union will accept it and the two countries can then work to eliminate nuclear weapons entirely, or 3. The U.S. can reply with a full attack but he will be forced to launch the rest of his weapons and both countries will be destroyed and possibly the entire world.

While the President is reading the message, S.A.C. Command is on the phone wanting the go codes for an attack, telling him one of the missile tracks is indicating a hit near the White House so he has less than five minutes to decide. Meanwhile the crew of the B-52 nicknamed "Polar Bear One" has been scrambled along with the rest of the flight on alert. The missile crew is popping lock to get their codes.

The novel is fast paced and takes place over a period of fifteen hours. It is well written with interesting characters. It gives a nicely done account of how things can spin out of control when critical decisions have to be made in the space of minutes and there is no time to weigh the factors involved. How much decision power is lost due to the speed of machines (computers) or the glitch that can occur? One of the points the President has to consider before the Premier's message comes in is that just weeks before a training tape was accidently loaded into a computer causing the alert personnel at North American Air Defense Command to have their on-alert screens tell them there was a Soviet attack being launched at the U.S. Good readers, this computer accident really happened.

If there is one annoying thing about the book it is that the author gets much of what happens with the plane and missile crews right but also gets almost as much wrong. I had the feeling that he watched the 1979 Air Force film *First Strike* and then several years later used his memory of that to help with the details in the book. It is a slight fault that can be forgiven and likely not noticed by a reader that doesn't have direct knowledge. Just so you'll know why it bothers me, I was a missile crewman during the time the novel takes place.

This brings to end the nuclear war section of our reviews. Next, we will be looking at books regarding what comes next, the aftermath.

# Alas Babylon

*Alas Babylon* by Pat Frank (Harry Hart Frank) will follow the theme of the last three chapters in dealing with the topic of nuclear war. Only now we are going to see takes on the aftermath of the conflict.

> "'Standing afar off for the fear of her torment, saying, Alas, alas, that great city Babylon, that mighty city! for in one hour is thy judgment come.'"
> - The Book of Revelation 18:10 - King James Bible

*Alas Babylon* is one of the defining novels of the late 1950s and early 1960s. Its view of the world and the United States is very much that of a small town and the people of that town. Pat Franks captures the feel of the era very well. His description of race relations and small-town life may make some people uncomfortable today but when he wrote the novel his outlook was very liberal. With those thoughts in mind, he creates an interesting, nicely written story. *Alas Babylon* was first published in 1959.

Pat Franks sets his novel in the small Florida town of Fort Repose. His main protagonist is Randy Bragg, a former army officer during the Korean War, a failed political candidate, and now a part time drunk/lawyer. Randy with his faults and an inclination to be lazy is still a likeable protagonist.

Our story starts with Randy going to the nearby air base to meet his older brother, Mark, who is a Colonel in the Air Force and the air intelligence officer for a General. Mark is worried that the world situation is falling apart and the chance of a war is growing stronger every day. In fact, he had Randy to meet him by sending a telegram that ends with the words "Alas Babylon," a code that the brothers had used since they were kids to indicate a situation of grave concern or impending disaster. At the meeting he asked Randy to meet his wife and kids at the airport later that night and get them to the relative safety of Fort Repose. The brothers part with the feeling that it's the last time they will see each other.

Randy returns to Fort Repose to make arrangements for supplies and comfort items for his soon-to-be arriving guests. In his time before their arrival, we meet the other people that will figure in the book. We also get a feel for the town and close by areas. Randy collects his sister-in-law, niece and nephew late that night and brings them to his house.

On the other side of the world events bring the pressure to a head and the worst-case scenario happens and the bombs start to fall. The people of Fort Repose are near enough to the air base to see the flash of the bomb that takes it out. Within hours the war is over. Fort Repose and Randy are isolated and the novel becomes a survival story instead of a war novel.

*Alas Babylon* reflects the thinking from the late 1940s and 50s of how a nuclear war would be fought and how it would affect the people and country of the United States. It is outdated in one sense. At the time it was written 90% of the nuclear bombs used would be dropped by aircraft with the rest coming from missiles. Also, the overall effects of the weapons are not as well-known as today. But it still remains a story well worth reading. I read the book over fifty years ago and it has stayed with me.

The novel is on many schools' reading list. It has had an influence on other writers and figures since its publication. John Lennon said it influenced his anti-war fervor. Authors David Brin and William R. Forstchen have both said that it influenced their post-apocalyptic novels. Give it a read.

# On the Beach

*On the Beach* by Nevil Shute is the second book in my reviews of after the nuclear happens works.

*On The Beach* is a post-apocalyptic novel written by British author Nevil Shute. In 1957 it appeared in the London weekly *Sunday Graphic* as *The Last Days on Earth* and was published as a full novel later that year. In it the nuclear war occurred a year before. The reasons for the war are deliberate attacks, mistaken identity of aircrafts, and land grabs, all of which result in the destruction of all civilization north of the equator.

To begin with, *On the Beach* is a very bleak story. Most of the bombs used in the war are cobalt enhanced, meaning that they produce great amounts of radiation lasting for years. All the fallout from the dirty bombs is swept around the northern hemisphere in months leaving no one alive. It also looks like the wind currents of the world are slowly bringing the radioactive clouds into the southern hemisphere. As we first meet the characters in the book the clouds of death have moved so far south that the only places left are Australia, New Zealand, South Africa, and the southern most part of South America.

Our central protagonist is Commander Dwight Towers, captain of the U.S.S. Scorpion a nuclear submarine and the last remaining U.S. military asset. He placed the sub and crew at the service of the Australians. His relationships with the people he meets in Australia allow us to know the many ways that they face the impending doom.

How will people face the end of the world? Party on, seek any way to survive a few days more, lay down and die now instead of later or in some other way? This is the real core of the novel. Shute helps you come to care for the characters in the book and brings you into their world. He gives you the same hope they feel when a radio signal in what may be Morse code is detected coming from the area of Seattle, Washington. Towers and his crew volunteer to sail into the deadly waters of the north to discover the source of the mystery tapping over the radio. No spoilers, remember.

Commander Towers and crew return to Melbourne where Towers picks up a friendship he had made with Moira Davidson. She is a very active woman and they fall in love. Bearing in mind the time the novel was written, Towers remains loyal to his wife. He also buys gifts for her and his children even though he knows there is absolutely no hope of them being alive. At one point talking with Moira, he asks her if she thinks he's crazy for doing that. She tells him no but I think she might have been wrong. In the world they are living in it would be very possible that all the doomed survivors tipped over the edge into at least a portion of insanity.

I highly recommend that you grab a copy of *On the Beach* and take the time to read it. It does take a reader into a world no one would want to find themselves in. It does reach you at a gut level and with the current climate of the world situation today it can give a reader the same chill those that grew up and lived under the shadow of nuclear war got over fifty years ago. Just be aware that it's not a cheerful evening read.

# One Second After

Continuing with the nuclear war theme *One Second After* scares the hell out of me. This novel by William R. Forstchen is a not so old and dusty tome. It was written in 2009 and updates the concept of the use of nuclear weapons in war outstandingly well. It didn't make a great splash with science fiction fans when it came out but did get to number eleven on the New York Times best seller list, performing well enough to have two follow up novels. What makes this piece more frightening than any other story of a nuclear war? Simple; it shows a new way to make war in an easy and terrifying manner.

What would happen if you took a small 65kt nuclear bomb and exploded it between 250 and 300 miles above the center of the United States?

The explosion would create an electromagnetic pulse (EMP) release that would cover the United States from coast to coast. The EMP would probably be strong enough to take out 90% of the electric power grids for the entire country as well as causing the failure of electronic devices including those in some cars, planes, and pretty much anything that uses electric power and is connected to the power grid.

Not a big problem you might think; after all we've had power blackouts in the past. So, everyone has to do without power for a few days ...no big deal. Alas the power would be gone not for days but for months, possibly years. The only time in recorded history something like it has occurred was the Carrington Event in September of 1859 when a massive solar flare struck the earth. Of course, there wasn't nearly the number of electrical devices in use then as there are now. But there were telegraph lines and the trans-Atlantic cable. The cable was knocked out and telegraph lines and offices caught fire

Imagine the chaos from an EMP: at a rough estimate about 16% of cars running at the time would go dead and never restart; No TV and radio stations would be on the air; and telephones, both land lines and cell-phone, would cease to function due to secondary effects. The car that didn't die would soon stop due to lack of gas – can't pump it with no power. Food distribution would become critical and pretty much disappear due to lack of ability to transport food. Modern cites both large and small are three days away from starvation. These are just the beginnings of the problems facing people in the aftermath of an EMP strike.

Which brings us back to *One Second After* for the hero of the book John Matherson, Colonel U.S. Army retired, has all these problems facing him. He had retired to a small town in North Carolina to teach at a college there. He is returning to his home when cars die and the TV and radio stations go off the air. He realizes very quickly what has happened from the clues he is getting. The people of the town discover that they are on their own and technology has dropped to a mid-nineteenth century level.

The challenges and moral issues that face the people in the book are hard ones. The author has done well at making the characters in his novel people that you like and want to see survive. He writes in a smooth flow that carries the reader along with ease. The novel is 350 pages and you wish it was twice that length just to see what happens to the people you come to know.

I'll leave you with one small semi-spoiler. The attack on the United States is due to a missile launch from a ship sitting in the Gulf of Mexico just outside the territorial waters of the U.S. We never find out who was behind the attack. It really doesn't matter; just the fact that one bomb and one missile could stop the entire country is frightening enough.

# Night of Camp David

Fletcher Knebel is best known for his political intrigue novels. *Night of Camp David* is one of the best of them.

It is sometime in the mid-1960s. Imagine that you are a junior senator from the midwest. You attend the Washington Press Banquet and have sat through the President's speech. In it were the usual jabs at the press and they were received well. But there was also an odd remark about the F.B.I. tapping all the telephones in the nation. The press and audience take it as a joke even though the President delivers it deadpan. There a few forced laughs and he finishes. You think it was just a busted joke. After all he's the President not a comedian.

You leave the event, return home, and have time to lose the tux for jeans and a sweatshirt. There's a knock at the door and its well after midnight. Wondering who it can be you open the door. Standing on the stoop is a member of the Secret Service Presidential detail. He immediately informs you that the President would like you to attend a meeting at Camp David. He tells you not to worry about changing, the President would like you to get there as soon as possible.

This is what happens to our hero, Junior Senator Jim MacVeagh. Once he arrives at Camp David, he goes to the Presidential lodge only to find the President standing in the darkened room of the cabin, only the light of the fireplace to illuminate the area. He then begins talking and gives a rambling narrative of his plans to unite the United States, Canada, and Norway to straighten out Europe. It comes out his joke of wiretapping the country was made as a serious remark. The poor Senator hears him out and is dumbfounded by it all. Before he can really comment on all of it, the President drops the other shoe. He has decided that the young senator is the perfect man to be his running mate in his reelection campaign in November.

As the book progresses, there are more meetings and by the time these have occurred the Senator is convinced that the President is profoundly paranoid and possibly mentally incapable of holding his office, He approaches his old friend and his wife to tell them what he thinks. Both of them think he is the one having a delusion.

What can he do? He is certain there is a madman with the ability to start World War III with a phone call sitting in the Oval Office. What would you do? What would anyone do? How could you convince other people that a man that appears to them to be perfectly sane and capable is actually stark raving mad?

This was an extremely difficult question to answer fifty years ago before Congress had written the guidelines for determining Presidential incapacity. Even today with the guidelines in place it would be a challenge to invoke them and to rule a President incompetent.

Knebel presents his hero with the dilemma. There are twists and turns all through which we wonder if he will find a solution. He also writes a tightly structured narrative. He maintains a pace that keeps you wanting to know the outcome. Will the hero convince people? Will the President go totally insane? Will the government fall? All these questions are answered and in the process the reader learns a few things about government and politics. Chase down a copy of the book and give yourself a treat.

I will warn you that you may get the feeling you are at the Hatter's tea party when talking about Washington D.C., for they're all mad there.

# Seven Days in May

Fletcher Knebel's novel *Seven Days in May* is his best and most well-known work. In it he combines his knowledge of world events and Washington politics into a gripping story. The novel was written and is set in the 1960s at the height of the Cold War. It was a New York Times bestseller for two months and made into a highly successful film.

Our protagonist is Marine Colonel "Jiggs" Casey who works for the Joint Chiefs. Casey has the Sunday duty shift at the Pentagon. He arrives at his office area and runs into one of the junior communication officers. The Comm officer makes a comment about how the Chairman of the Joint Chiefs, Air Force General James Scott, is as bad as the enlisted men running a betting pool on the outcome of the Preakness next Sunday. Casey is amused by the story but tells the Lieutenant he might think about not talking about a four-star general's betting pool. Casey takes the message about the bet, wads it up and places it in his trouser pocket.

When Casey tells story about the message to the General, there is an odd reaction from him. General Scott dismisses it and tells Jiggs to forget about it. The day passes with no more incidents. The message remains forgotten until Casey leaves for the day and finds the wadded-up paper in his pants as he heads home.

Jiggs had a dinner party later in the evening. While he is attending it, he overhears a comment made by a senator talking to a small group of men. This causes a raising of an eyebrow as the conversation is about a forthcoming top secret military drill that should be known only to the Joint Chiefs and himself. As he mulls this over, things click and he connects the dots that the drill and the Preakness are happening at the same time to the hour.

The next day, Monday, he learn that a flight of planes belonging to a unit called ECOMCON are to fly into Washington from a base in Texas, neither of which he has any knowledge of existing. Casey brings this up with General Scott. Scott tells him that he must have missed the paperwork when it passed over his desk. Later in the day, Scott tells him he thinks he may be overworked and should take a few days off.

Several more odd things turn up for Casey to see including running into an old friend that is stationed at the base in Texas. They visit and more unknown facts are revealed to Casey of things going on that he should know about but doesn't. At that point Casey begins to really investigate. He slowly comes to believe that there is a plot to overthrow the government of the United States. General Scott is planning to replace the President who he has disagreed with over a disarmament treaty with the Soviet Union.

The book from that point is a fast-paced story that doesn't let up. It is well worth reading if only for the study of the relationship between the military and the civilian elements in our country at the time the story was written.

The character of General Scott is thought to have been based on General Edwin A. Walker who did actually have severe disagreements with President Kennedy and later resigned under pressure. It is also possible that the storyline may have been based on a real incident from the Roosevelt administration.

Grab yourself a copy and sit back for a couple of hours of fun reading. Then catch the movie version written by Rod Serling (avoid the 1994 remake *The Enemy Within*; redeemed only by Dana Delany and Forrest Whitaker in lead roles.)

# Dr. Strangelove: or How I Learned to Stop Worrying and Love the Bomb

Peter George is an author reviewed earlier in the nuke war series of reviews for his novel *Red Alert*. He's back for *Dr. Strangelove: or How I Learned to Stop Worrying and Love the Bomb* (hereafter referred to as *Dr. Strangelove*) for simple reasons. First and foremost, it is a good book and second it was based off *Red Alert*. It's also a break from the seriousness of the nuke, crazy president, and junta stories because it's a comedy. A black comedy but a comedy nevertheless for you still get drunken world leaders, crazy generals, and military power.

When film director Stanley Kubrick got interested in the mutual assured destruction doctrine, he started reading about it and found it mad in the sense of insane. He also worried about the ability of anyone to keep control of the weapons that could destroy mankind. In his reading he ran across *Red Alert*. He thought that it would make a good film. He and Peter George put their heads together and a screenplay was created but as they worked the dead serious novel turned into a satiric comedy.

Peter George left the movie process before filming started but did decide to write the novelization of the first draft script. It's that version of Dr. Strangelove that is the subject of this chapter.

As in *Red Alert*, the motivating factor is an Air Force General that has slipped a cog; only this time it's General Jack D. Ripper. It's also where we get to see the fun Peter George has with names as he follows up by introducing us to Group Captain Lionel Mandrake, U.S. President Merkin Muffley, General 'Buck' Turgidson, Major 'King' Kong, Russian Ambassador Alexi de Sadesky, Russian Premier Dimitri Kissof, Colonel 'Bat' Guano, and most especially Dr. Strangelove. His playing with names even runs to inanimate objects in the story.

The story progresses much the same as the events of *Red Alert* but more outrageous and overboard as the tension builds over impending nuclear war. The humor runs from subtle to broad slapstick, especially the parts dealing with Dr. Strangelove's alien hand syndrome. This is a real syndrome and can have some of the effects mentioned in the novel.

Peter George's novel is as funny today as when it was written and holds meaning for today as the world drifts back toward the possible hell of a nuclear exchange. It is a book you can laugh at but it can also plant the seed of thought that pops up as you laugh, "What the hell am I laughing at, this could really happen. Some damn fool could start a nuclear war. For real." Hopefully that's the power of the book, to make the people reading it stop and think of how foolish men can be and the dreadful consequences of letting the nuclear genie out of the bottle.

We've been holding back the nuke demon for almost eighty years now. With a little luck and a lot people pushing for it maybe just maybe we can find a way for our grandchildren to live without a nuclear sword hanging over their head.

# The Dollar Series

This particular series came about in an odd way. It all starts with a pulp story by Dashiell Hammett- *Red Harvest*. Which inspired Akira Kurosawa to make his 1961 film *Yojimbo*. That in turn inspired Sergio Leone to make *A Fistful of Dollars*. That led to a novelization of the movie followed by the same for the next two movies. The books sold well enough to become a series of eight over the years after the first one was released. The first and fifth books in the series were written by Frank Chandler and Brian Fox in that order. Chandler's novel read like the movie script with little development of the characters or addition to the story line. Fox also has a lack of catching the spirit of the Man with No Name. Joe Millard, the third author in the series, writes his Dollar novels in a nice style and manages to get the feel of the character and the humor in the stories as well.

Millard has a good flowing style of writing that makes the books quick, fun reads and a good way to relax for a couple of hours after a long day. While the series does come from the movies, Millard, by the time he wrote *The Good, The Bad and The Ugly,* made the nameless man his own. The novels add to the background of the man known as Senior Ninguno, Nameless, No Name, The Stranger, The Hunter, The Bounty Killer, Americano, and Mister Sudden Death. All terms that reference the hero or anti-hero (depending on how you view him) in the novels.

While we do learn more of his background story, we never do learn his name. But that's just as well for if we did, he would lose some of the conundrum surrounding him. The enigma wrapped in a poncho can be a cold-blooded killer yet can save a girl and show great kindness. He isn't a white hat nor a black hat; mostly he's a grey hat. For the readers that are gamers, he's chaotic good.

The books came indirectly from a pulp story and they have a pulp feel to them since they have a steady flow of action and are fast paced. If the Man with No Name had been around in the golden age of pulps, I think he could easily have had a following to keep a magazine running for several hundred issues. Alas we only have the eight novels listed here:

*The Good, the Bad and the Ugly*
*A Fistful of Dollars*
*For a Few Dollars More*
*A Coffin Full of Dollars*
*A Dollar to Die For*
*The Devil's Dollar Sign*
*The Million-Dollar Bloodhunt*
*Blood for a Dirty Dollar*

    The list is chronological for the timeline in the books. You might notice that the first book is *The Good, The Bad, and the Ugly* and if you're a fan of the movies you're thinking that it's out of order. The movies should be watched in the same order that the books are listed. *The Good, The Bad, and the Ugly* takes place during the Civil War and there are graves in the cemetery marked 1862 and 1864 so it must take place sometime between 1864 and 1865. *A Fistful of Dollars* has a grave marked 1873 and *For a Few Dollars More* has a newspaper archive dated 1873 so they must take place in 1873 or later. And yes, I do play movie and book trivia. The books after the movie books seem to follow the timeline as described. But the novels can be read in any order and it doesn't hurt the fun in any way.
    The books aren't easily found but can still be bought at used bookstores and other places. Grab a couple and sit back and relax with a brief trip to the old west.

# The Time Machine Stories from *Boys' Life*

Long ago way back in December of 1959 I got an extra birthday present. I was a good scout and working on merit badges and of course reading *Boys' Life* and there in the December issue was a story called 'The Day We Explored the Future', the very first Time Machine story in a series. The issue by chance arrived on my date of birth that was a Friday that year. I wish I could say I remembered that it was a Friday but I looked up the calendar for December 1959. I do remember reading the story and loving it.

For the next eight years or so it was always fun to find a Time Machine story in the latest issue to turn up in the mailbox. The stories were written by Donald Keith, who actually was a father/son team named Donald and Keith Monroe. They would write over eleven stories when I was reading the magazine and I was pleasantly pleased to discover that they would continue to write then until 1989 for a total of twelve more. The last few were written by Keith alone.

In 'The Day We Explored the Future' two scouts Bob Tucker and Ellsworth 'Brains' Baynes are biking through the desert on the way to their Scout Camp and Bob takes them on a short cut down a canyon he's always wanted to explore. As they go along, they spot a metallic object partly buried in a rockslide. Of course, being fairly normal scouts, they have to check it out and soon discover it's some sort of saucer shaped machine.

Brains, the device loving one of the scouts, wants to get inside it and soon they find a hatch. In they go and Brains begins to fiddle with the dials and gauges he sees and then notices a lever that he pushes forward. The machine start to hum and lights flicker. The hum rises to a high pitch and then the machine appears to die. Bob is less than thrilled by the machine doing something and tells his buddy so and they scramble for the now reopening hatch. The two scouts discover that the rock slide has fallen off the machine. Bob realizes that their bikes are missing.

Brains put two and three together and determines that the device is a time machine and they've gone forward in time. As they are discussing this development a group of what appears to be cub scouts come marching toward them. Only these cubs are completely bald and have very large heads. Bob and Brains soon attempt to communicate with the group and find they are speaking a very strange form of English. The Scoutmaster of the group thinks they are giants and renders them unconscious. They wake up in a future zoo.

They are shortly befriended by one of the future Boy Scouts named Kai. He helps them escape and wants to return to the past with them. During the escape the boys and Kai wind up separated, but they finally make it to the time machine. Brains starts working the lever again. Back to the past they go and poor Kai is left behind. Bob and Brains tell no one about the machine and contemplate returning to rescue Kai.

The boys and the time machine have many more adventures over the next thirty years. The stories are fairly short but well written and even years later hold up well. They are written on a juvenile level but the style does become more adult as the years go by for the boys and the real world. The first stories are collected in two books <u>Munity on the Time Machine</u> and <u>The Time Machine to the Rescue</u>.

The good news is both books can be found and the first runs are reasonably low in price but the second book is somewhat uncommon, so it can run to and sometimes over 100 dollars. That was the bad news but the good news is there is an online archive of *Boys' Life* where they are free to read:

https://media.boyslife.org/archive/#issue=UUksHG783IcC

For those that decide they want to read the stories, here's a list of the issue dates and story titles:

DEC 1959 "The Day We Explored the Future"
FEB 1960 "The Time Machine Flies Backwards"
JUN 1960 "How We Got the Mind-Reading Pills"
JUL 1960 "Our Time Machine at the Jamboree"

OCT 1961 "Marco Polo and Our Time Machine"
FEB 1962 "The Time Machine Slips a Cog"
DEC 1962 "Mutiny in the Time Machine" Dec 1962 to Mar 1963 (4-part serial)
JUN 1964 "The Time Machine Cracks a Safe"
OCT 1964 "Time Machine to the Rescue"
FEB 1965 "The Time Machine Gets Stuck" FEB 1965 to Apr 1965 (3-part serial)
APR 1967 "The Time Machine Hunts a Treasure" APR 1967 to Jun 1967 (3-part serial)
DEC 1968 "The Dog from the Time Machine"
SEP 1970 "The Time Machine and the Generation Gap"
AUG 1971 "The King and the Time Machine"
FEB 1973 "The Time Machine Cleans Up"
AUG 1973 "The Time Machine Twins the Jamboree"
DEC 1973 "Santa Claus and the Time Machine"
NOV 1974 "The Time Machine Fights Earthquakes"
APR 1975 "The Time Machine Saves a Patriot"
JUL 1976 "The Time Machine Kidnaps a Parade"
SEP 1988 "Target Timbuktu"
FEB 1989 "Why We Kidnapped Our Scoutmaster"
SEP 1989 "Pirates Took Our Time Machine"

# Harry Bates and Don A. Stuart

This week's dusty tomes are two stories by authors Harry Bates and Don A. Stuart. The stories may not have been read by many of my readers, especially the younger readers, i.e. the ones under thirty and possibly the ones under forty.

So why two stories instead of novels? As I said, a number of readers may have never run across the stories but the stories have had an impact on the larger scope of science fiction and the reader that hasn't run across them have likely seen the movies made from them. The titles are *Who Goes There?* (1938) by Don A. Stuart and *Farewell to the Master* (1940) by Harry Bates.

As I said most current readers unless they go looking for older collections of golden age science fiction stories will not know these tales. So why should they seek out these to read? First, both are well crafted stories that are well worth reading just for the entertainment value. Second, they are groundbreaking stories if only for their impact on the science fiction culture in the 1950s.

Both of the writers were editors of *Astounding* Magazine during its earlier years and during the golden age. Harry Bates had been the editor during the mid-thirties and Don Stuart would helm the magazine through the golden age and well into the start of the new age writers in the late sixties and early seventies. With that very blatant hint I'll reveal that Don A. Stuart was a pen name for John W. Campbell.

Bates isn't as well remembered for his editing of *Astounding* as he is for his writings. John W. Campbell on the other hand is most remembered for his editing of the magazine. He introduced and guided the hand of most of the authors that we associate with the golden age. Heinlein, Clark, Asimov and H. Beam Piper to name just a few of the people are those he brought to the readers of science fiction in the 1940s. Campbell is given a great deal of credit for the start of modern science fiction.

Harry Bates did have a successful career as a writer and was published in many of the pulp magazines in the 1940s. He remains a fairly popular author until the late 1950s. Every once in a while, one of his novels will come back into print though they don't remain out very long. Campbell, while well remembered as an editor, is almost forgotten as a writer and this is not too surprising as he was a much better editor than a writer. But if either man had written nothing but the two stories above, they would still be well thought of as writers.

*Farewell to the Master* is a more thoughtful piece than an action piece. It is one that will pull you into the story and keep you interested and after you read it you will think about the story later. I try to avoid spoilers but here's a short blub to the story. A craft from another world lands on the earth and a visitor emerges to greet the people of Earth. This all happens before the story actually starts.

*Who Goes There?* is more of an action story and moves rapidly. Once again, we have an alien visitor to the earth but this time the visitor is hostile. While this story will also make you think, it will also scare you.

You will find your reading time well spent if you track these stories down and read them. I'll let my readers that haven't been around for years and years or become a seeker of old masters in on why these stories had a great impact on the science fiction culture. In 1951 both stories were made into movies. *Farewell to the Master* became *The Day the Earth Stood Still* and *Who Goes There?* became *The Thing from Another World.* Both would be hits and still hold status as classic science fiction movies today. The written stories are classics as well, so do yourself a favor and track them down online and read them.

# H. Beam Piper

This time a trio of books by Henry Beam Piper, eerr, Horace Beam Piper, ahh err H. Beam Piper.

H. Beam Piper was a writer from the late 1940s to the mid-1960s. We lost Beam in 1964. If he had lived his name would have been in the same class as Heinlein, Asimov and Bradbury. I know you're wondering about the name in the lead to the chapter. The simple fact is no one is really sure what Beam's first name really was. Some of the confusion came from Piper himself. He liked to tell some interesting tales in his books and with his friends. His Para-time stories were fan favorites and involved parallel worlds. He told the story he was really from a parallel world but when he got here there was already a writer named H. B. Fyfe and he changed his name to H. Beam Piper. He was so good at telling the story and keeping a straight face about it that some people began to wonder if there might be some truth to it.

In this chapter I'll be discussing the three novels for which Beam Piper is most well-known. These would be *Little Fuzzy*, *Space Viking*, and *Lord Kalvan of Otherwhen*. These three come and go out of print on a fairly regular basis, about every twenty years or so, and I haven't seen any of them on a bookstore shelf a good while. They are three books a well-read science fiction fan should read and it you just like a fun adventure, they work as that too.

I would be placed in a hard spot it I had to choose my favorite of the three. At any given point in the day, I might say *Little Fuzzy* and later in the same day say it was *Space Viking* and there is also a lot of special appeal to *Lord Kalvan of Otherwhen*. Since that's the way they came out, I'll review then in that order.

Jack Holloway is a miner on the planet Zarathustra looking for sunstones. He's doing a good job of finding them when one day a small critter wanders into his camp. It's small, has fuzzy hair and he watches it hunt a land prawn using a stick to flip and kill it.

Before the day is over Jack has become Papa Jack and the critter is given the name Little Fuzzy by him. Over the few days he and Little Fuzzy adopt each other and the little guy even brings his family into Jack's camp to live.

Jack continues to observe the fuzzies as he calls all of them and slowly comes to believe that they are intelligent creatures. This gives him a problem in two ways: if they are, then the sunstone hunting will stop since there is a government that will protect the planet for its indigenous people and knowing the Zarathustra company that buys the stones will be very unhappy about the loss of a great fortune. *The Fuzzy* stories answer these two questions and bring up more that lead to two sequels. The third Fuzzy book was lost for almost 20 years. Its recovery by a fluke of chance makes for a good con story. You'll love the Fuzzies and if you become a Piper fan the Ewoks may really annoy you since they do bear a strong resemblance to Fuzzies.

Our second Piper book is *Space Viking* which has the spirit of a rip-roaring space opera. The story takes place in the far distant future. Long before the events of the novel there was a vast Terran Federation of planets. When a great war occurs in the Federation a large number of refugees fled beyond its boundaries to found what have become the Sword worlds, a loose collection of worlds bound together in a feudal system of kingdoms, duchies, and other small states. They often war against each other and have recently received word that the old Federation had fallen apart and many worlds once a part of it have regressed into primitive cultures. This leads some of the Sword worlds to raid them for old technology and wealth much as the Vikings would raid into Europe during the Viking Age.

But our story is that of Baron Lucas Trask, who is about to marry Elaine Karvall, the love of his life. Just before their wedding is to take place Andray Dunnan, an insane man who believes the bride is being forced into the marriage, declares his love for Elaine and tries to get her to flee with him. She attempts to reason with him and show him he's wrong but he goes into a rage. He crashes into the wedding and kills her and seriously wounds Lucas.

The novel tells the tale of how Lucas seeks his revenge against the madman. It has action and adventure enough to please any fan of both. It's a fun and easy read and a great way to spend an evening.

For our third Piper experience, allow me to take you on an adventure with Corporal Calvin Morrison of the Pennsylvania State Police. Corporal Morrison with another trooper is about to capture a wanted criminal when a strange vehicle appears before him and takes him inside. The driver of it reaches for a weapon and the Corporal beats him to the draw doing a roll across the floor to take cover. In doing this he rolls right on out of it to the hard ground. The strange machine disappears and he finds himself all alone.

Calvin rises to his feet realizing as he does that the cabin he and the other trooper were about to enter has disappeared as well as the other trooper and their patrol car. He slowly comes to the conclusion that something is wrong with the very land around him. The terrain is no longer the land he knows. He's surrounded by old growth forest and even a mining cut on a mountain side has disappeared. The story only gets more interesting from that point.

Calvin has been transported to a parallel world. He discovers that the people in this new world speak a language he has never heard and their technology is hundreds of years behind his world. Even more he discovers he's fallen right into the middle of a war. The kingdom he's in is about to have to fight with its neighbors because it is under the sway of priests of the god Styphon. Styphon is the god in control in these kingdoms or at least his priests are since they are in control of the secret of making fireseed. Fireseed or what we would call black powder determines what kingdom will win wars. But there's a new factor in the soon to come war- Corporal Calvin Morrison also know how to make gunpowder. How the Corporal becomes Lord Kalvan is a story well worth the read.

If you run across me at a con stop and chat and we talk about Piper's stories, and I'll tell you the story of the lost Fuzzy novel and the tragedy of H. Beam Piper.

# Medal of Honor

Mack Reynolds was a very good science fiction writer from the 1950s to the 1980s. He passed from the scene far too early. His works spans the major themes of science fiction from time machines to Interstellar warfare. There were many other themes that he touched on and many he conceived that have been used by other writers or come to pass in the real world.

Reynolds was a veteran of World War II so it is not surprising that several of his stories are connected with warfare in space. *Medal of Honor* was a longtime fan favorite. I recall nice reviews at the time of its first publication in the November Issue of *Amazing*.

I was lucky enough to read this story in a third hand, possible fourth or fifth hand copy I found when I was a teenager. It stuck with me from then until now as a good story. And it is a good story, not just from the content story of winning the medal but from the writing aspect as well. It is a well-crafted story that holds the reader's interest throughout. The pace is a steady pull to the end and has enough action to keep a reader just looking for a fun read as well.

Having said all that, it also has some damn interesting ideas to put forth involving the average Joe, heroes, success, and **The Medal**. It is a thinking story and a precautionary tale in more than one way.

The Medal is important in the history of the Solar union. Only 36 men have won it, only eight didn't receive it posthumously and four pages into the story the last living winner dies. The protagonist of the story will be the next to wear **The Medal**. The unique thing about this medal is that the winner can do no wrong and is so admired that he can't even give money to a beggar much less pay for anything. It's all on the house for him.

Space Scout flier Don Mathers thinks that to win **The Medal** would be great provided you survive with your skin and other bodily functions intact. Only thing is he hates his job of space scout in the one-man ship. He also is close to a mental crack up from the stress looking for the aliens that invaded the solar system fifty years ago and the weeks of solitude in space doing the looking. If he can just find a way out of the military, life would be better.

It might be difficult to find a copy of the *Amazing* issue the story was published in, but it has appeared in a few anthologies as well a collection of Reynolds stories. Even if you can't find it all hope is not lost. In 1976 Reynolds expanded the story into a novel retitling it *Galactic Medal of Honor*.

In its new incarnation the story doesn't lose anything and possibly gains more depth. As an example, in the novel **The Medal** has only been won twelve times and of those times only four were not posthumously so that Don becomes the thirteenth winner. Again, the information that this is in the space of fifty years comes out but now we know that the first twelve awards were all given for actions occurring in the first and only battle with the aliens so far.

Having both the original story and the novel to read and compare is well worth it for the reader just for the enjoyment and for other writers to see how to lengthen a story without watering it down and making is a lesser story. Do yourself a favor and find one of the versions and have a fine time reading it. I should also add that in checking my dates for the chapter I read through a list of Mack's stories and discovered that there were quite a few that I have missed reading and you can count on my looking for them to read. I also discover that I had forgotten that he was also the first writer to do an original novel from *Star Trek* (original series) – *Mission to Horatius* - and did it while the show was still airing. It was done as a youth novel for Whitman, basically a big little book of the sixties and as I recall not the best written of the Whitman TV novels. I have it on my shelf with the James Blish script adaptations and will be rereading it soon.

# Kelly Freas

Kelly Freas was, if you go only by awards, the best science fiction artist ever. He won the Hugo ten times and so far, no one has come close to matching this record. His artwork and illustration set a high mark for others to try for. The old saying is you can't judge a book by its cover but, good readers, at least once in a while you can.

I miss his cover art. Freas was able to give his artwork for books and stories a style that made the people in the work real. They have character and he let his sense of humor come through as well. I only had the pleasure of meeting and talking to Kelly Freas for a way too short five-minute period at a world con many years ago. But standing in line to get a signed print you could see the twinkle in his eye and the fun he had in talking with fans.

I do wish it was possible to show you the covers I plan to discuss as they sit on my shelf. After all, a picture is worth a thousand words. I'll give a couple of comments on why I miss his work on covers and illustrations today, citing those just behind me.

First up is his idea of Poul Anderson's character Nicholas van Rijn from the very first story about him. Freas captures van Rijn.

> "He was a huge man, two meters in height and broad enough to match. A triple chin and swag belly did not make him appear soft. Rings glittered on hairy fingers and bracelets on tawny wrists, under snuff-soiled lace. Small black eyes, set close to a great hook nose under a sloping forehead, peered with laser intensity."

The Freas cover actually tells you some of the story while the book cover for the later novel just says here's a sci-fi novel. You can see the posters on the wall behind the man in the first cover. Looking closely, you see the left poster is for a theatrical performance and the right poster is for could be an election and that all three male faces resemble each other. The book cover is a guy standing at a spaceport and a big head above him. Again, which would you pick to read? Seek out the images online, tell me if I'm wrong.

I could continue with covers for a long time since Kelly Freas literally did several hundred covers. Kelly Freas is well known for more than just his science fiction and fantasy work. He did 50 *Mad* magazine covers of Alfred E. Neuman. During World War II he was stationed in the Pacific as a reconnaissance camera man and did nose art for bombers in his spare time.

So good readers, you might just buy a book for its cover.

# The Space Willies

Eric Frank Russell was a British author who wrote primarily for an American audience. He has a smooth easy reading style to his writing. His works cover both science fiction and fantasy. There is a story that's been around for a long time that John Campbell started *Unknown,* the sister magazine to *Astounding,* just to publish Russell's story *Sinister Barrier*. The story is most likely apocryphal.

Willies by definition means to have a fit of nervousness for no real reason, as in, "That dark room gives me the willies." Back when I was a young lad this was a common expression but I haven't heard it in a long while so I thought I should define it. My favorite Russell novel is *The Space Willies.*

Russell's story has appeared under three titles. When it was in *Astounding* as a novella it was called *Plus X*. Then in the British full-length novel it was called *Next of Kin*. And finally in its American appearance as a novel the new title is *The Space Willies*. I'm not sure why the book appeared under three different titles but I think that the original title may have been the last one. My idea is that it began with the *Astounding* title coming from John Campbell who would change titles when he thought he had a better one. The Ace books published the novel in 1958 we got *The Space Willies*. Then with the British publication Russell would have had a problem getting the book out under that title in Britain since willies there would have brought a different picture to mind. In Britain the word willy is polite slang for the male genital organ. *The Space Willies* is a far better title for the novel than either of the others.

The story is just plain fun. The hero of the book John Leeming is just the type of guy that fans in the fifties and sixties would have loved. Like a great number of his counterparts in other books, he's a true smart ass and thinks that he's more intelligent than most people. He also has a very cavalier attitude toward authority and following rules, very much like the readers back in that time period.

There is a war on between humans and an alien empire of which little is known. How big it is, how many worlds, and so much more needs to be known, but how do they find out? The answer is simple; give Leeming a pilot of one-man scout ships a new unarmed ship with a special engine that makes it faster than any other ship around; have him go deep into the enemy's space lanes and discover as much as he can then send the information back; finally hit the drive hard and escape back to home space. Simple unless you do the scouting and send the info and then the engine goes putt putt and you crash on an enemy world.

That's where the story really begins. Our hero is umpteen billions of miles from home and totally surrounded. All he has to do is survive and steal a ship and scoot for home. A truly great plan until you contact the enemy and he captures you. Now what? I won't spoil the ending for the reader but you can guess that it will involve Space Willies.

Eric Frank Russell was not only a good writer but was also one of the early science fiction writers to have a great comedic touch. He would write many novels with a great deal of humor in them. I can't say that the book will give you space willies but it will give you space giggles. You might not find the book in your local book store but it can be fairly easy to locate a copy. I would hope that you do. It may hopefully lead you to having to find other stories by Russell.

# Last Man Off Wake Island

This chapter is being written the day after Memorial Day. I had two Marine relatives, my Uncles Calvin Stephens and Gene Seales. Uncle Calvin was a World War II Marine and Uncle Gene was a Korean War Marine. Calvin passed away at age 91, just 11 days before Memorial Day. He didn't see the battles that are covered in this week's book but did see Iwo Jima and the end of the war. Gene was the one that passed several of his childhood books on to me when I was a kid and one of them was Col. Bayler's book.

Both my uncles were in my thoughts Memorial Day and my only set plans was to eat dinner with my daughter, so in the morning I pulled *Last Man Off Wake Island* down from the shelf and reread it for the twentieth plus time. I came home and decided to just relax and watch a movie. I scrolled through the channels and discovered not too surprisingly to me that what little history relating to the day was being shown I had seen more than once. I thought well maybe there was a movie worth the time to watch. Again, no luck, so time to hit my DVD shelf. Having just reread *Last Man Off Wake Island* the one I put in the player was *Wake Island*.

I got to thinking I'd bet I could pick the first fifty people I saw under the age of thirty-five and if one of them recognized the name Wake Island I would be amazed and if they could tell me anything about the battle, I'd faint.

Thus, a little history lesson begins. On December $7^{th}$, 1941 the Empire of Japan attacked the United States. Hopefully most know about the air attack at Pearl Harbor but at the same time as Pearl was being hit there was an invasion force and air attack headed to Wake. Wake Island is a small spot in the Pacific Ocean located 2.452 miles west of Hawaii. It's so far west you cross the International Date Line going there.

On December $7^{th}$ ($8^{th}$ on Wake) there were 449 Marines, sixty-eight sailors, five U.S. Army personnel, and about 1,200 civilian workers to defend the island. They had twelve fighters, six five-inch coastal guns, twelve three-inch anti-aircraft guns and forty-eight machine guns to fight with. Bombing started the first day of the battle after which the number of fighters were down to 4. On the 11$^{th}$ the first invasion landing took place. Coming at the Marines were three light cruisers, six destroyers, two patrol boats, two troop transports, and 450 Special Naval Landing Force troops.

| **Results that day:** | **Marines** | **Japanese Forces** |
|---|---|---|
| | 1 KIA | 2 destroyers sunk |
| | | 325 sailors KIA |
| 2$^{nd}$ landing 23 Dec. | 52 killed | 2 transports sunk |
| Includes all for battle | 49 wounded | 2 patrol boats wrecked |
| | 2 missing | 7–8 aircraft shot down 20 damage |
| | 433 captured | 320 killed - 333 wounded estimate |

For fourteen days the Marines and the others including civilians that jumped in to help withstood the Japanese attacks. The last message sent from Wake read, "Situation still in doubt."

Col. Bailer tells the story of the first part of the battle. He was ordered off the island before the second landing. The book was published in 1943. As you can tell from the cover the story was told to Cecil Carnes, who put the book together. Carnes was a war correspondent. He does a fair job of conveying the story but he wasn't Ernie Pyle, so some of the feel of being there is lost. But the book is well worth reading for the first-hand account of the battle. There are other books and articles by the men who survived the battle and even tales from those who were Prisoners of War for the remaining years of the war after the battle.

*Last Man Off Wake Island* has become hard to find and a good copy can be fairly expensive. A detailed account of the battle can be found at

https://www.nps.gov/parkhistory/online_books/npswapa/extcontent/usmc/pcn-190-003119-00/sec1.htm

Earlier in the chapter I mention the movie of the battle, *Wake Island*. Production for the movie began before the real battle was over and was released in August of 1942. It was a smash hit for the year and William Bendix got his only supporting role Oscar nomination for it. It is overly romanticized but was something the American public needed after the aftermath of Pearl Harbor.

Friends, readers, and brother Marines; Semper Fi!

# If the Universe is Teeming with Aliens ... Where is Everybody

For those readers not familiar with the Fermi Paradox I'll give a brief explanation. In 1950 the great physicist Enrico Fermi was walking to lunch with several other physicist friends and they got into a discussion about a report they had seen of a recent UFO sighting. The conversation moved on and the scientists had started eating when Fermi suddenly asked, "Where are they?" This drew a general laugh and they all knew he was speaking about extraterrestrial life. Fermi then did some calculations on the probability of intelligent life in our galaxy, leading him to wonder why we had not had contact with them or why they had not covered the galaxy by that time.

In 1961 Dr. Frank Drake would come up with the following:

$R*$ – the average rate of star formations in our galaxy,

$fp$ = the fraction of formed stars that have planets,

$ne$ = for stars that have planets, the average number of planets that can potentially support life,

$fl$ = the fraction of those planets that actually develop life,

$fi$ = the fraction of planets bearing life on which intelligent, civilized life, has developed,

$fc$ = the fraction of these civilizations that have developed communications, i.e., technologies that release detectable signs into space, and

$L$ = the length of time over which such civilizations release detectable signals,

$N$ = equals the number of planets with intelligent civilization in our galaxy.

$$N = R \times fp \times ne \times fl \times fi \times fc \times L$$
Drake's Equation

Using low estimates for most factors the equations give a number as low as 20 and possible as high as 1,000,000 planets with intelligent life. That would be calculating with the information we had about the universe at that time. Redoing it with current information gives both a lower and higher number. Either way we come back to Fermi's Paradox, Where Are They?

In *If the Universe is Teeming with Aliens ... Where is Everybody?*, Stephen Webb takes on the task of giving us some answers. He gives a very good background of the history I short-handed earlier. He then discusses the Fermi Paradox and Drake's Equation. In his writing, the ideas and principles are explained for a non-science reader and easily understood.

In his very entertaining book, he has fifty short chapters that offer solutions to the Fermi Paradox. In each he explains why it either is not a true solution or shows how it fails to answer the paradox. Not all of the solutions are his work, and he gives credit to whoever devised the answer originally.

In the last chapter entitled "THE FERMI PARADOX RESOLVED..." he gives his own solution that he hopes answers the paradox. I'll avoid a spoiler here and let you read the book for yourself to see if he has come up with the solution. You'll be glad I did. If you have an interest in the Fermi Paradox and the possibility of intelligent life out there, you'll want to read his book just for the fun of it.

Webb's book is well written and his thinking on the paradox well-reasoned. One thing I liked about the book is he includes a chapter on notes and further reading to do about the paradox. I'd like to list one other book here that he didn't have in his list due to it being published after his was written. I highly recommend to you *The Eerie Silence* by Paul Davies. Both of these books are well worth the reading.

I'll close with a paraphrase from I believe Arthur C. Clark, "Either we are alone in the Universe or we are not. Either way it scares the hell out of me."

# The Writers of Star Trek

*Star Trek*; were you there on September the 8$^{th}$ 1966? I was and fell into a love of the *Star Trek* universe that hasn't faded. It's that fascination with the dream of a great universe and world filled with hope, a sense of wonder, and the belief that we as a species can be better than we were then and are now.

I was already an avid reader of science fiction. I opened the TV guide preview issue and saw that there were several such shows coming in the new season. Here's a list of the names of the ones that would fall under a loose heading of science fiction. Coming on ABC – *Dark Shadows, The Green Hornet,* and *The Time Tunnel*; CBS – *It's About Time*, NBC – *The Girl from U.N.C.L.E., Star Trek,* and *Tarzan*. Also, the local station and the only station in town at the time started running *Lost in Space, The Man from U.N.C.L.E.,* and *Voyage to the Bottom of the Sea*.

I watched all of them but *Trek* was the Show. I really liked *The Man from U.N.C.L.E.* and *The Green Hornet*, but none of them stuck like *Trek*. I could name episodes, quote lines, and name the actors. I can still do it. I was thinking on this after chatting with my best friend a couple of weeks ago (Yep, Rick, still hanging in there and you can still be the science office as long as I get the Captain's chair.) Why did *Trek* stand out to us so much? Yes, there was the dream but something else had to key in as well. Thinking on it I realized one major factor was the writing and then keying off that I started to think that there well several well know science fiction writers of the time that wrote episodes of the show, not to mention the very excellent adaptations of the scripts that James Blish turned into a collection of twelve books of short stories. Speaking of Blish, he was both a Hugo and Nebula award winner and if you haven't read his *Cities in Flight* stories you should. The stories have great depth and meaning to them.

Checking on the writers of the *Trek* episodes I did find that there were several known science fiction writers. I also decided to look at any list I could find online of the best *Star Trek* episodes and found a large number.

Now would be a good time to make a list of your top ten episodes before reading any further. This isn't required but you might have more fun and get to compare your list to the others that you'll read later in the chapter.

I started doing a little math with them and then decided to get my own list of top ten Trek episodes. A call was sent to friends and some fellow writers for their top ten lists of Trek episodes as well. I took their list and the online lists and did a little math with them. Not all lists had the same episodes in their choices and some were only on one list, both for the critic/online reviews lists as well as the friends lists. You may find the information gleaned from it in the following: Episodes are listed from one to ten with one being the best or most favorite episode. Here come the lists, last chance to make your own list before they start.

Critic/online lists   * episodes indicate pro science fiction writer

| Episode | rank | score |
|---|---|---|
| The City on the Edge of Forever* | 1 | 8.75 |
| Balance of Terror | 2 | 6.75 |
| Mirror Mirror* | 3 | 5.75 |
| Space seed | 4 | 4.875 |
| The Trouble with Tribbles* | 5 | 4.375 |
| Amok Time* | 6 | 4.25 |
| The Doomsday Machine* | 7 | 4.0 |
| Arena* | 8 | 3.75 |
| Journey to Babel | 9 | 2.87 |
| The Enemy Within* | 10 | 1.25 |

Friends/writers   *episodes indicate pro science fiction writer

| | | |
|---|---|---|
| Balance of Terror | 1 | 9.5 |
| Amok Time | 2 | 8.75 |
| The Trouble with Tribbles* | 3 | 8.625 |
| Arena* | 4 | 5.5 |
| The Enemy Within* | 5 | 4.37 |
| Space Seed | 6 | 4.35 |

| | | |
|---|---|---|
| The City on the Edge of Forever* | 7 | 4.25 |
| Mirror Mirror* | 8 | 3.75 |
| Where No Man Has Gone Before | 9 | 2.91 |
| The Doomsday Machine* | 10 | 2.50 |

Combined results 11 on list due to two episodes not on both lists

| | | |
|---|---|---|
| Balance of Terror | 1 | 8.12 |
| The City on the Edge of Forever* | 2 | 6.5 |
| Amok Time* | 3 | 6.005 |
| The Trouble with Tribbles* | 4 | 6.000 |
| Mirror Mirror* | 5 | 4.75 |
| Arena* | 6 | 4.12 |
| Space Seed | 7 | 4.61 |
| The Doomsday Machine* | 8 | 3.25 |
| The Enemy Within* | 9 | 2.81 |
| Where No Man Has Gone Before | 10 | 1.45 |
| Journey to Babel | 11 | 1.43 |

## My Top 10

| | |
|---|---|
| Balance of Terror | 1 |
| Space Seed | 2 |
| Mirror Mirror* | 3 |
| Amok Time* | 4 |
| The Doomsday Machine* | 5 |
| The Trouble with Tribbles* | 6 |
| Arena* | 7 |
| The Enemy Within* | 8 |
| The City on the Edge of Forever* | 9 |
| Requiem for Methuselah* | 10 |

How did your list compare? Here are the science fiction writers that did episodes. An * indicates a Hugo award winner:
Jerome Bixby
Robert Bloch*
Shimon Wincelberg
Richard Matheson
Fredric Brown
Harlan Ellison*

Norman Spinrad
David Gerold

The rest of the figures I got are these:

There are nine known writers that did more than one episode. Between them they wrote sixteen episodes.

20% of the *Trek* episodes were written by known science fiction writers. This is more than any other show, in or near the time period *Star Trek* aired that I could find with the next closest being *The Twilight Zone* with 13%.

60% of the top ten were written by them on the critic list.

70% of the top ten were written by them on the friends/writer list.

80% of the top ten were written by them on my list.

On both the critic and friends lists all ten came from the first and second seasons and I have the outlier with one from the third season.

The writers that didn't win a Hugo were at some point nominated for it or received a Nebula award or nomination.

Basically, these guys knew how to write and helped make Star Trek the show we love. You can find many of their books and stories still in print. Give all of them a try.

Special thanks to Ginger Oh Snap, Richard Jones, Jonny Byrd, Cliff Easley, Dale and Jim Hingle. Stephen Howell, Charles and Diane Welshans and all the rest that sent lists.

# The Greenwich Village Hippies Trilogy

Once upon a time, long ago, in a distant, wondrous age vaguely remembered as the sixties, in a season called love, in an odd little kingdom named Greenwich there lived an odd group of beings named Hippies. Three members of this happy little collection were friends and they were a magician, artist, reporter, musician, war protester, and a writer (I know that's more than three types but these guys were talented.) The writer talked the other two into writing as well which led to our trilogy. Good readers, allow me to introduce you to Chester Anderson, Michael Kurland and T. A. Waters and the Greenwich Village Trilogy made up of their three books *The Butterfly Kid*, *The Unicorn Girl*, and *The Probability Pad*.

Chester Anderson is headed through the Village when he notices the kid walking toward him; nothing unusual about him, he looked more or less like all the other new arrivals up until you noticed him making a fist and every time he did it a butterfly appeared in the hand as he opened it. So begins the first chapter of *The Butterfly Kid*. Ok hopefully from this you've guessed that the author of the book and the protagonist of the book are one and the same. Shall I say that the book gets stranger from this point. After all it is the sixties and we are dealing with hippies. Sort of, kinda…the book proposes to be set in the future but anyone in 1967 knew it was happening then and had friends that matched some of the supporting characters.

What can possibly happen to a group of kind hearted hippies in the early days of 1967 after all the summer of love was just ahead? How about the kid, the reality pills, and an invasion from space by giant alien lobsters. It's up to Chester, Michael the Theodore bear, and Tom Water to save the world and have a damn good time while doing it. I'll speak no more of it after all we're here and the world is here so they must have succeeded ---right?

Yes, yes because *The Unicorn Girl* takes place only a couple of months later and they are all back and we're all here. But life is about to take another weird shift for them. For suddenly there are fire breathing dragonets, mean metal tanks, freaks and fuzz, the most beautiful girl in the world and of course the Unicorn Girl. But those problems and people come later. It all started when Tom Waters disappeared. Not to0 unusual since he is a magician except it the wrong kind of disappeared, he was really gone. Searching for him is when Michael sees the Unicorn Girl and things start to happen. Time to save the world again. Once more I have to say no more of it; after all we're here and the world is here so they must have succeeded ---right?

Sure, sure they did. *The Probability Pad* happens just a few months after the just mentioned oddities. This time it's T. A. Waters that has the problem. Chester has vanished, oh wait that was a mistake there is a double of Chester running around…hang on a minute there's a duplicate for everyone they know bouncing around the Village. Oh no it's that time again. The boys have to save the world again. Will they succeed?

The three writers do a great job of writing the books. I enjoyed them when I read them many years ago and got as good of a kick out of rereading them for the chapter. All are quick reads as well as being a blast of fun and the writers weave a running story that entertains through three books. They do write them so well you wish that the trilogy was a series and have run for at least a few more books with our hippy heroes. The only drawback about the books is getting a copy to read now. They can be hard to locate and if you do the price is a tad high, around eighty a book as an average price and sometimes breaking the hundred-dollar mark. I believe there is an eBook of *The Butterfly Kid* going for much less. Grab the e copy to start the series and then talk to friends and see if there is a copy you can borrow or attend a few science fiction conventions and dig through the used book tables. It'll be worth it.

**Peace and Love my brothers and sisters!**

# Theodore Roosevelt

This chapter's books deal with a man that lived life to its fullest; a man who became larger than life to his fellow countrymen. T.R., Colonel, and That Damn Cowboy, are all names that refer to Theodore Roosevelt. They all apply to him in many ways. You may notice I didn't list Teddy as one; the Colonel didn't like the nic name so it will not be used.

There are more books about TR than I can list here. I chose the two I cover for the following reasons. Both are enjoyable and fairly quick reads and both are well worth the time it takes to read them. Also, they happen to be the ones on my shelf. In the process of reading them you'll learn a little about the sickly child that became a robust man of the West (as in the old West) and who would go on to be one of the greatest Presidents of the United States.

Our first book, *American Boys' Life of Theodore Roosevelt* was written by Edward Stratemeyer, who some of you may know better under his pen names such as Victor Appleton, Franklin W. Dixon, Carolyn Keene, and Roy Rockwood. Yes, good readers the person responsible for the Hardy Boys, Nancy Drew, and Bomba the jungle boy wrote many biographies of historical and contemporary figures.

If you have read any of his young adult novels from the series mentioned here, you would know as well as me that the writer knows how to keep your interest. He is brief in some instances in this biography but does cover TR's life well. I do have to admit that the book is incomplete in the coverage of the latter part of Roosevelt's life. This is only because the book was published in 1904 while Theodore was still in his first term as President. There is a little hero worship in the reporting of Roosevelt's life in this book. Of course, I kind of think he deserves it.

Let's discuss our second volume, *The Rough Riders*, and I have to confess this is an older book as well. It was published in 1899 but gives an intimate knowledge of TR and his time in service during the Spanish-American War. This might be easy to understand since the book was written by Lt. Colonel Theodore Roosevelt. This wasn't Roosevelt's first book nor would it be his last. I found the book to be written by someone conversant with the use of the English language and not afraid to use it.

Colonel Roosevelt begins the book with a dedication that is most fitting.

> "ON BEHALF OF THE ROUGH RIDERS
> I DEDICATE THIS BOOK
> TO THE OFFICERS AND MEN OF THE
> FIVE REGULAR REGIMENTS
> WHICH TOGETHER WITH MINE MADE UP
> THE CAVALRY DIVISION AT SANTIAGO"
> Theodore Roosevelt

Have no fear good reader for the Colonel does cover the charge up San Juan Hill.

I can recommend both books to you and highly encourage you to read them. You can't go wrong discovering the remarkable man who set the tone for the Twentieth century and started the United States on the path to becoming a world power; at the same time he began the National Parks of our country and lent his name to a still favorite toy of many children. That's correct the much beloved Theodore Bear is named for him.

For those of you that would like to delve deeper into the life of Theodore Roosevelt I highly recommend the biographical trilogy written by Edmund Morris. But buy the books one at a time; you might strain something carrying them home as all three volumes run to the neighborhood of 1,000 pages. If you enjoy movies, I would also suggest watching *The Wind and the Lion* in which Brian Keith has the role of President Theodore Roosevelt. He gives an excellent performance and catches the nature of the man.

Bully sir, Bully! Read for a man needs knowledge.

Chapter 47

# Time For Rhyme

Notes on three authors and an introduction to the manly art of poetry.

Sometime after the 1940s to now there has been a lack of poets, especially in the science fiction and fantasy writing. The only contact most readers have to poems is the brief and lackadaisical touch of poetry they get in the way it is presented to them in school classes, for we must read the great poets and carve them apart to see how they wrote the great works for which they are known. No wonder when that and the 1950s view of manly fortitude were combined writing poetry fell into a black hole.

May I introduce you to these gentlemen:

I would think that most of my good readers have heard of at least two of these poets. Just in case I'll give each a brief introduction.

Rudyard Kipling was an English author who wrote novels and poems that are still being used by Hollywood today as in the latest version of *The Jungle Book*. Kipling was held in high esteem during his lifetime and many thought he should have been the poet laureate of the British empire. He was the first English writer to win the Noble prize for literature.

Here's a few lines of his verse to give you a feel for his writing.

From *Barrack-Room Ballads*

"Gentlemen-Rankers"
To the legion of the lost ones, to the cohort of the damned,
To my brethren in their sorrow overseas,
Sings a gentleman of England cleanly bred, machinely crammed,
And a trooper of the Empress, if you please.
Yea, a trooper of the forces who has run his own six horses,
And faith he went the pace and went it blind,
And the world was more than kin while he held the ready tin,

But to-day the Sergeant's something less than kind.

>We're poor little lambs who've lost our way,
>    Baa! Baa! Baa!
>We're little black sheep who've gone astray,
>    Baa—aa—aa!
>Gentlemen-rankers out on the spree,
>Damned from here to Eternity,
>God ha' mercy on such as we,
>    Baa! Yah! Bah!

Some of you may have heard this one as a song.

From *The Jungle Book* "The Law of the Jungle"

>Now this is the Law of the Jungle -- as old and as true as the sky;
>And the Wolf that shall keep it may prosper, but the Wolf that shall break it must die.
>As the creeper that girdles the tree-trunk the Law runneth forward and back --
>For the strength of the Pack is the Wolf, and the strength of the Wolf is the Pack.

Kipling wouldn't forget to bring in history.

From *Puck of Pook's Hill* "A Pict Song"

>Rome never looks where she treads.
>Always her heavy hooves fall
>On our stomachs, our hearts or our heads;
>And Rome never heeds when we bawl.
>Her sentries pass on--that is all,
>And we gather behind them in hordes,
>And plot to reconquer the Wall,
>With only our tongues for our swords.
>We are the Little Folk--we!
>Too little to love or to hate.
>Leave us alone and you'll see

> How we can drag down the State!
> We are the worm in the wood!
> We are the rot at the root!
> We are the taint in the blood!
> We are the thorn in the foot!

You may have heard it as a song as well. Leslie Fish released it as a filk song many years ago.

Robert W. Service lived the life of an adventurer. He was a Canadian writer and was there during the gold rush in the Yukon. His poems of the sourdough miners and their lives are great to read. He also fought in the Great War as one of the bravest and most dangerous roles a man could take, a Red Crossman or what today we call Corpsmen, if you're a Marine, or a Medic for the other services. Here are a few lines from the Yukon days and the war.

From The *Spell of the Yukon* "The Cremation of Sam McGee"

> There are strange things done in the midnight sun
> By the men who moil for gold;
> The Arctic trails have their secret tales
> That would make your blood run cold;
> The Northern Lights have seen queer sights,
> But the queerest they ever did see
> Was that night on the marge of Lake Lebarge
> I cremated Sam McGee.
>
> Now Sam McGee was from Tennessee, where the cotton blooms and blows.
> Why he left his home in the South to roam 'round the Pole, God only knows.
> He was always cold, but the land of gold seemed to hold him like a spell;
> Though he'd often say in his homely way that "he'd sooner live in hell."

That's one of my favorites from Service and it's on my bucket list to actually sit by Lake Labarge in the Yukon and watch the

Northern lights. Ahh maybe next year but until then we'll just have to read a few lines from his time in World War I.

> From *Rhymes of a Red Cross Man* "Only a Boche"
> We brought him in from between the lines: we'd better have let him lie;
> For what's the use of risking one's skin for a tyke that's going to die?
> What's the use of tearing him loose under a gruelling fire,
> When he's shot in the head, and worse than dead, and all messed up on the wire?
> However, I say, we brought him in. Diable! The mud was bad;
> The trench was crooked and greasy and high, and oh, what a time we had!
> And often we slipped, and often we tripped, but never he made a moan;
> And how we were wet with blood and with sweat! but we carried him in like our own.

Service does well at catching the sadness and desolation of war. That said, let's move on to an American writer. Robert E. Howard is most likely known to you. After all, he created an iconic character in fantasy. Yes, the writer of the Conan stories also wrote poetry. Here's a few lines of his to enjoy.

> "John L. Sullivan"
> Bellowing, blustering, old John L.
> Fearing nothing 'tween sky and hell!
> Rushing, roaring, swinging his right.
> Smashing, crashing, forcing the fight.
> Battering foes until they fell,
> Tilt your glasses to old John L.!
> Mitchell he knocked, from the ring clear out!
> Dropped Kilrain with a single clout!
> Laflin he beat and Burke he flayed,
> Knocked out the Maori Giant, Slade!
> Packed in each fist, damnation and hell!
> Tilt your glasses to old John L.!

Shall we put in a little Howard magic to the mix.

"Forbidden Magic"
There came to me a Man one summer night,
When all the world lay silent in the stars,
And moonlight crossed my room with ghostly bars.
He whispered hints of weird, unhallowed sight;
I followed – then in waves of spectral light
Mounted the shimmery ladders of my soul
Where moon-pale spiders, huge as dragons, stole –
Great forms like moths, with wings of wispy white.
Around the world the sighing of the loon
Shook misty lakes beneath the false-dawn's gleams;
Rose tinted shone the sky-line's minaret;
I rose in fear, and then with blood and sweat
Beat out the iron fabrics of my dreams,
And shaped of them a web to snare the moon.

We must bid the English gentlemen and the Texas roughneck farewell until we next pick up one of their books, for now it's time to fall back a thousand years. It's 1048 c.e. and a baby is born in the ancient land of Persia. His father was not of royal blood. In fact his last name was Khayyam (the tent maker); he would be named Omar and become a world-famous mathematician, astronomer, philosopher, and last but surely not least, a poet. He would become known by the name Omar Khayyam. While famous in his time it would not last, let's leave Omar in 1109. We shall move geographically to the land that William the Conqueror had made his own just a few years before that, but in time we shall travel a thousand years.

We have arrived in the year 1809 c.e. in the English town of Suffolk. Another baby boy is born, given the name of Edward Purcell; his father married well and took up the name and arms of his wife's family. So, Edward became a Fitzgerald, and this made him an heir to great wealth and able to pursue what he wished in his adult life. He too, like Omar, would grow up to be a writer and poet. But he became a translator, who dove into translating the poetry of Omar. If he had not become fascinated with it, neither he or Omar would be well known in the western world. Without further ado I give you the words of two men that still bring joy, hope, and deep thinking to us.

*The Rubaiyat of Omar Khayyam*
>  Here with a Loaf of Bread beneath the Bough,
>  A Flask of Wine, a Book of Verse - and Thou
>  Beside me singing in the Wilderness –
>  Ahh Wilderness is Paradise enow.
>
>  The Moving Finger writes; and, having writ,
>  Moves on: nor all thy Piety nor Wit
>  Shall lure it back to cancel half a Line,
>  Nor all thy Tears wash out a Word of it
>
>  Ah, my Beloved, fill the Cup that clears
>  TO-DAY of past Regrets and future Fears -
>  *To-morrow ?* - Why, To-morrow I may be
>  Myself with Yesterday's Sev'n Thousand Years.

Most of the poems quoted are not the full-length poems and there are many more like them as well as many other writers from the golden age of science fiction and fantasy who wrote poems. Good readers, do yourself a great favor and go find some of works of poetry by these and other writers. It will increase your soul and stir your blood. If some of you still believe that there's nothing to learn from poems, I suggest you go read "The Truce of the Bear" by Kipling; I think you may find that it goes along with the world today.

TAMAM SHUD

# The TV Books Part I

Back in the dark ages when I was a teenager of around fifteen years old, my favorite TV shows premiered. My readers that are too young to remember anything before 1979, let me share with you that there was indeed a time that you only got to see an episode of your favorite shows one or two times; once on the first broadcast and hopefully a second time on the summer reruns of the show. Then it was gone forever unless the show remained on the air long enough (usually five years or more) to be put into syndication. That only helped you if your local station (there were many towns that had only one TV station) decided to purchase your show. Also, until the late 1960s to early 70s cable was not common for many areas.

But all was not lost. It was very common for a book based on a popular show or movie to written or even for the TV show to be based on an existing book series. The likely number of books from the show was usually small, around one to three.

In this first chapter of tv book remembrances, I'll introduce you to the TV series book that broke that mold. I give you - *The Man from U.N.C.L.E.*

United Network Command for Law and Enforcement is a secret agency fighting against crime worldwide. Its main target, the most efficient and largest group the Network deals with, is THRUSH. THRUSH, or as it revealed in the book series, Technological Hierarchy for the Removal of Undesirables and the Subjugation of Humanity, was founded by Colonel Sebastian Moran after the death of Professor James Moriarty from the Sherlock Holmes books. By the time We are learning about both groups THRUSH is composed of many Nazis and worse criminals from around the world.

Our main heroes are agents Napoleon Solo and Illya Kuryakin, polar opposites in many ways. Solo is an American and Kuryakin is Russian. Solo is calm, logical, and easy going. Kuryakin is quick tempered, brilliant, but somewhat reserved. Both are highly intelligent. They have a strong admiration for each other and a desire to make their world a better place. This played well with the public who saw in it the hope that the U.S. and the U.S.S.R. might someday have a similar relationship.

There was a third man (small joke that those of a certain age will get) who helped the overall feel of the interplay with comment to the two heroes and gives depth to the U.N.C.L.E. world. Mr. Alexander Waverly is the head of U.N.C.L.E. and sends the two agents on their assignments. Mr. Waverly is an Englishman and he looks more like an Oxford professor with his tweed coat and pipe than a deadly player in a world-wide chess game for the lives of many people.

We get to learn more about the men of U.N.C.L.E. in the books. There are twenty-four books as well as twenty-four magazines, two Better Little Books, a single-issue slick magazine, and a book supposedly written by the U.N.C.L.E. agents: The ABCs of Espionage.

There was also a spinoff, *The Girl from U.N.C.L.E.* which also had two books stateside and a monthly magazine. There is also an unpublished twenty-fifth book in the book series. All books and magazines (including the twenty-fifth book) can be found on the internet archives. To get printed copies could easily cost several hundred dollars to acquire.

**The Man From U.N.C.L.E. Books**
*The Man from U.N.C.L.E.* (a.k.a. *The Thousand Coffins Affair*) by Michael Avallone
*The Doomsday Affair* by Harry Whittington
*The Copenhagen Affair* by John Oram
*The Dagger Affair* by David McDaniel
*The Mad Scientist Affair* by John T. Phillifent
*The Vampire Affair* by David McDaniel
*The Radioactive Camel Affair* by Peter Leslie
*The Monster Wheel Affair* by David McDaniel
*The Diving Dames Affair* by Peter Leslie
*The Assassination Affair* by J. Hunter Holly

*The Invisibility Affair* by Thomas Stratton (Robert Coulson and Gene DeWeese)
*The Mind Twisters Affair* by Thomas Stratton
*The Rainbow Affair* by David McDaniel (cameos by The Saint, Miss Marple, John Steed, Emma Peel, Willie Garvin, Tommy Hambledon, Neddie Seagoon, Father Brown, a retired Sherlock Holmes (aged nearly 100), and Dr. Fu Manchu)
*The Cross of Gold Affair* by Fredric Davies (Ron Ellik and Fredric Langley
*The Utopia Affair* by David McDaniel
*The Splintered Sunglasses Affair* by Peter Leslie
*The Hollow Crown Affair* by David McDaniel
*The Unfair Fare Affair* by Peter Leslie
*The Power Cube Affair* by John T. Phillifent
*The Corfu Affair* by John T. Phillifent
*The Thinking Machine Affair* by Joel Bernard
*The Stone Cold Dead in the Market Affair* by John Oram
*The Finger in the Sky Affair* by Peter Leslie
*The Final Affair* by David McDaniel (Never published)

**The Girl From U.N.C.L.E. books**
*The Birds of a Feather Affair* by Michael Avallone
*The Blazing Affair* by Michael Avallone
*The Global Globules Affair* by Simon Latter (published in U. K.)
*The Golden Boats of Taradata Affair* by Simon Latter (published in U. K. only)
*The Cornish Pixie Affair* by Peter Leslie (published in U. K. only)

# The TV Books Part II

For this series we must travel to a small town on the coast of Maine. The mist rolls in from the sea. Soon the sun will set and the shade of evening will join with the fog to envelop Collinsport with shadows, dark shadows. At Collinwood lights come on with night fall, a strange eerie chill embraces the mansion. For this is indeed *Dark Shadows*.

Its 1966, all across the country housewives dropped what they have been working on, college students headed to their dorms, and teenagers rushed home from school, to turn on the tv and plop in a chair waiting for 4 o'clock to see the swirling mists and crashing waves that are the opening to ABC's new afternoon soap opera *Dark Shadows*. I'm included in those teenagers rushing home. As I recall at this distant date from 1966, I saw an article in TV Guide that a new show was coming on that was gothic in nature. Being a fan of science fiction, fantasy, and the Universal monsters I figured I might like it. I can't say that it became a passion for me at that point, but I did keep up with the show over the next few weeks. Then came the fateful day Barnabus Collins was introduced. Wow a show with a vampire, Monday through Friday. Yep, I was hooked.

Just like the *Man from U.N.C.L.E.*, *Dark Shadows* had a fan base that couldn't get enough of the characters even with it being on every weekday. But this was a soap opera so no summer reruns and in those times soaps didn't get syndicated. Any new fans missed the background that had been built and were lost to it unless a friend had watched and could fill them in on the strange happening at Collinwood.

One day though I was checking out the arrivals at my favorite book seller, when I spotted on the shelf the first of what would be many novels in the Dark Shadows universe. That first book started with Victoria Winters heading to Collinsport and then continued with the story and had new story lines as well.

**The Dark Shadows series**
Published by Paperback Library author of all books was Dan Ross writing as Marilyn Ross.

*Dark Shadows* December 1966
*Victoria Winters* March 1967
*Strangers at Collins House* September 1967
*The Mystery of Collinwood* January 1968
*The Curse of Collinwood* May 1968
*Barnabas Collins* November 1968
*The Secret of Barnabas Collins* January 1969
*The Demon of Barnabas Collins* April 1969
*The Foe of Barnabas Collins* July 1969
*The Phantom and Barnabas Collins* September 1969
*The Peril of Barnabas Collins* November 1969
*Barnabas Collins and the Mysterious Ghost* January 1970
*Barnabas Collins and Quentin's Demon* February 1970
*Barnabas Collins and the Gypsy Witch* March 1970
*Barnabas, Quentin and the Mummy's Curse* April 1970
*Barnabas, Quentin and the Avenging Ghost* May 1970
*Barnabas, Quentin and the Nightmare Assassin* June 1970
*Barnabas, Quentin and the Crystal Coffin* July 1970
*Barnabas, Quentin and the Witch's Curse* August 1970
*Barnabas, Quentin and the Haunted Cave* September 1970
*Barnabas, Quentin and the Frightened Bride* October 1970
*House of Dark Shadows* October 1970
*Barnabas, Quentin and the Scorpio Curse* November 1970
*Barnabas, Quentin and the Serpent* December 1970
*Barnabas, Quentin and the Magic Potion* January 1971
*Barnabas, Quentin and the Body Snatchers* February 1971
*Barnabas, Quentin and Dr. Jekyll's Son* April 1971
*Barnabas, Quentin and the Grave Robbers* June 1971
*Barnabas, Quentin and the Sea Ghost* August 1971
*Barnabas, Quentin and the Mad Magician* October 1971
*Barnabas, Quentin and the Hidden Tomb* December 1971
*Barnabas, Quentin and the Vampire Beauty* March 1972

2nd series publisher HarperCollins

*Angelique's Descent* Lara Parker December 1998
*Dreams of the Dark* Stephen Rainey & Elizabeth Massie October 1999

3rd series publisher Tor Books

*The Salem Branch* Lara Parker July 2006
*Angelique's Descent* Lara Parker (a prequel to *The Salem Branch*) 2012
*Wolf Moon Rising* Lara Parker August 2013
*Heiress of Collinwood* Lara Parker November 2016

*Dark Shadows*, like *The Man from U.N.C.L.E.* before it, would have great success with the novels, comic books, and movies, including an attempt to reboot the show as a primetime show with new actors in the roles and would be number one in book series and other venues, if not for the show that I'll continue with in the next chapter.

# The TV Shows Part III

We have reached the number one show, both for me and in terms of book series. It came to life in 1966. It was somewhat of a magic year. Many of the new shows on tv that year still have a following and are found even now in syndication on many stations. Here is a list of the ones that I still have fond memories of and will sit and watch if I catch one scrolling through channels looking for something to watch: *Mission Impossible, Dark Shadows, The Monkees, The Green Hornet, The Girl from U.N.C.L.E., The Time Tunnel*, and *The Rat Patrol*. All had novels and comic books based on them published when they were still on the air and some had movies made then. Some had movies made in the past few years and a couple had attempts to reboot the show with new casts. But when talking about success in novels that sprang from television shows- The all-time winner is *Star Trek*.

How? Oh, let me count the ways. First let's get the non-written material taken care of; several of the other shows had reboot attempts that didn't succeed, After *Star Trek* was canceled, it did reboot to tv. Granted it was as an animated series but the original actors voiced their characters in the series and several of the scripts used were ones chosen for the original series that didn't get made. The first Trek book was published during the series' original run. The first book series would run for thirteen books, the first twelve simply called *Star Trek 1-12*. They were written by James Blish, a well-known science fiction writer, and J. A. Lawrence. In total Blish would write twelve Trek books. Of those eleven were stories adapted from the tv series scripts plus a standalone novel (first original novel for adults) that was published in the middle of adapting the scripts; there was a children's novel written during this time as well. Number 12 in the script's adaptations would be written by Blish and J. A. Lawrence. Unfortunately, Blish would die while working on the remaining adaptations and his wife J. A. Lawrence would complete the ones scheduled for book 12. That would still leave two original episodes left. J. A. Lawrence would adapt both *Mudd's Women* and *I, Mudd* as well as writing a new Harry Mudd story under the title of *Mudd's Angels*. *Mudd's Angels* is the thirteenth book and is normally listed with the other books. While the adaptations continued the animated series began and shortly after that Alan Dean Foster would adapt the scripts from that series in a ten book series named *Star Trek Log 1-10*.

*Star Trek* fans were delighted. *Trek* was off the air but we could read the original adventures again anytime we wished. Meanwhile new *Trek* novels were being released. As of this writing there are well over 250 *Trek* novels feathering the original show crew.

Just as a side note: while *Trek* never got the hoped for return to the air a few years after the last original air-the return of the tv show became *Star Trek the Motion Picture)-The Next Generation* and subsequent shows served as both reboot and continuation. McCoy, Scotty, and Spock appear; Harry Mudd popped up in *Discovery*; and in the current *Star Trek* spin off *Strange New Worlds*, so far we've seen Kirk, Spock, Scotty, and Uhura; not to mention that Captain Pike and Number 1, both of whom were seen in the original series.

Those of you that are *Star Trek* fans and haven't read the books, give them a try. They are the same but in the Blish books he adds to the background and personalities of the crew. As an example, in the adaptation of "Balance of Terror" Captain Kirk is about perform a wedding at the start of the show. In the Blish story he reveals that Kirk is tone deaf and doesn't recognize the wedding march being played. Side note: any fan that has heard William Shatner's album recorded when *Trek* was on the air will have no trouble believing that Captain Kirk is tone deaf. The Blish books are easily found in used bookstores or on ebay where you can also find the stories in the form of four hardback books (you'll still have to find the paperback edition of the Harry Mudd episodes.)

To wrap, what a success *Star Trek* was after the original show. There have been numerous movies, comic books, tv spin-offs and the novels for every show number over 850.

There is a world of good Trek stories out there. Go read as much as you want.

# Live Long and Prosper!

# Doomsday Plus 1

As I write this, it's around 2:15 a.m. since I like writing late and sleeping late into the morning. At the same time in the desolate spaces in the middle of our country, there are eighty young Air Force officers forty feet underground. Their ages range from twenty-three to around thirty-two and most are $1^{st}$ and $2^{nd}$ Lieutenants with a sprinkling of Captains and maybe a few Majors thrown into the mix. One is sleeping and the other is sitting in a chair with aircraft seat belts on it. The officer is listening to a soft flow of air that cools the equipment around the chair and for the sound of a message coming over the radio that stays on always or one of the other communication devices in the equipment. The officer is the Deputy Combat Crew Commander and until 20 minutes ago the DCCC had been sleeping. Now the Combat Crew Commander is the one in the small bed.

The rest of the eighty are doing the same thing with a few variations. They are all on alert at one of the forty Launch Control Centers located across four states in the upper middle of the U.S.; the LCC's are manned 24 hours a day, 365 days a year and have been for over five and a half decades. The LCC is connected with 10 Minuteman Missiles armed with either the W78 (335-kiloton yield) or the W87 (300-kiloton yield). The crew is there for one reason; should the radio or other communication equipment deliver them a valid message both will go to a red ¼ inch steel safe welded to the wall. On the front of the red box are two 4-digit combination locks. the CCC knows the combination for one lock, the DCCC knows the other. They will pull out a document that validates the part of the message. Each will also remove a key with a tag labeled CCC or DCCC. The keys are inserted into launch switches far enough away from each other so no one can reach both at the same time. They then strap into their chairs with eyes glued on the LCC clock waiting for the time from the message to be reached (easier to tell the time now that they have a digital clock;

the last time I stood alert it was a seven day manual windup clock.) As the time gets near both have their hands on the keys, the CCC counts 3-2-1-mark! They both turn keys as do all the other missileers. 400 MMM's are away.

Thirty minutes later somewhere halfway around the world 400 targets (enemy airfields, missile silos, military bases, cities, and people.) are struck. At the same time submarines are launching their missiles and Bombers are in air to drop their bomb hours later. And, boys and girls, that is how civilization, millions of people, huge amounts of animal and plant life disappear in mere hours and if enough bombs go boom everything, including the earth, dies.

Doomsday – the missile crews, submariners, pilots, you, me, and all the other people don't like to think about it. Every January the *Bulletin of the Atomic Scientists' Science and Security Board* set the hands on the Doomsday Clock. In January of 2025 they moved the hands closer to midnight. The clock is set to 1 minute and 29 seconds to Midnight. That's the closest they have been to midnight since 1947.

What to do when midnight arrives? If you live in a major city, near major bridges, military bases, rail centers, missile sites, or live in one of 1,931 cities, towns, and villages with populations over 10,000 you could be a target. You can improve your odds by moving where the incoming sorties will not be hitting. Let's say that Doomsday arrives from another cause; super earthquake or volcano, asteroid strike, or a true black death plague. Time to be a boy scout; be prepared.

There are a lot of people that do some kind of prepping. What do you put in your bug-out-bag is a fun game for conventions and there are a lot, I mean a lot of videos and books upon books on the subject to be found. When I go to sci-fi/fantasy/gaming conventions or several miles from home I don't have a bug out bag but I do have a get home bag.

For this chapter I thought I'd recommend a few books to read that will fit right in with the scenarios I just set up. Over all the ones I've picked give a good idea of life after Doomsday and do have some good ideas for those prepping to survive it.

I'm starting with a novel that dates back just after World War

II. In 1941 George R. Stewart wrote a novel called Earth Abides. A great plague has swept the earth; ninety percent of the population of the planet has died. Ish is a graduate student in geography working on his master's thesis. He's in a lonely spot in the Sierra Nevada. While working to get a rock sample he is bitten by a rattlesnake. He grabs his gear and the hammer he was using and stumbles to the shack where he's been staying. He drops into his bed and develops a fever and notices he has apparently contracted measles as well. Several days go by while he burns with the fever. Weakened but finally able to get out of bed, he decides to go home. As he is driving it appears to be a holiday. No one is on the road and he does not see a soul when passing through a small town.

By the time he reaches his home in Berkeley, California, he realizes that he may be the last man on earth.

Beyond telling you that he isn't the last human, no spoilers here. The book follows Ish as he strives to re-establish civilization. *Earth Abides* is a good solid read. It has recently been made into a TV series which I haven't seen so I can't say if it is good but the novel is well worth you spending a couple of hours reading.

We now travel forward in time to 1959. This brings us to the still early days of the Cold War. Pat Frank writes a novel, *Alas Babylon*. I covered this novel in an earlier chapter so I will not go into deep details on it. I'll repeat that it is good reading, and I'll tell you how I was introduced to it.

The book was a hit, and the very well-respected live drama TV series *Playhouse 90* selected it to be adapted for the small screen. It was broadcast April 3, 1960. I was 10 years old and to this day 65 years later I can still remember watching it. I can recall scenes as vivid as if I were again sitting in my parents' living room seeing it on our black and white 20" screen TV (we had a big one.) It had an impact then and a couple of years later when I ran across the book I got the same kind of impact from it.

The book does have some good ideas for what to do if the bombs drop. An added note; this was on the shelves and on the air just a little over a year and a half before the very real Cuban Missile Crisis occurred. With that, we will leave happy days of the fifties and continue into the sixties.

We are going to stumble through the rubble to 1962. This is the year of the missiles of October. The U.S.S.R. puts missiles in Cuba just 90 miles from the U.S. coast. President Kennedy and Chairman Khrushchev would play a game of brinkmanship for 13 days, neither man having all the facts of the crisis to work from. No one at the time would realize how close we came to nuclear war. Here's the way it was put at the time by then Secretary of State Dean Rusk: "We're eyeball to eyeball and I think the other fellow just blinked." It would be after the fall of the U.S.S.R and classified documents were released that the world would know that the missiles in Cuba were fully operational and one man stopped a Soviet submarine from sinking U.S. ships in the blockade of Cuba.

If you want more and better information about the crisis, I highly recommend you check out these books;

*13 Days* by Robert F. Kennedy
*The Missiles of October: The Declassified story of John F. Kennedy and the Cuban Missile Crisis* by Robert Smith Thompson
*Essence of Decision* by Graham Allison
*One Hell of a Gamble* by Aleksandr Fursenko and Timothy Naftali.

A couple of the books have been made into excellent movies as well.

July 5, 1962; school has been out for a month and summer still seems to be endless. I was lucky enough to be able to go to work with my dad. Dad was the co-owner of a cab company in my hometown but an hour after I was there boredom sat in and I was ready for adventure. In other words, I could wander around downtown and see what was happening. In those long-a-go days it was fairly safe for a 12-year-old kid to do that, not to mention that two of my uncles were part-time drivers at the cab company and all the drivers knew me. Also, one of my good friends from Boy Scouting's father was the chief of detectives for the police department so most of the cops knew me as well. So off I went to the library, the bookstore, the five and dime stores on $5^{th}$ street, all of which wasted a couple of hours. Back to the cab company and ten minutes later I was bored again and on that lucky day I was given fifty cents to go to an afternoon movie, straight out the door to the end of the block and across the street to the Temple Theater. I have no idea what was playing there but it didn't catch my interest.

Across the street again and one block east I hang a left and on the right-hand side of the street was the Royal Theater and on the left-hand side was the Rebel that ran second releases, usually a double feature on the weekend but Saturday was days away and I had seen what was showing. So, the Royal it was. As I reached the front, I saw the framed poster for the movie that just opened, *Panic in the Year Zero*. Oh boy, a science fiction movie. In I went, one quarter spent. A soda and a box of popcorn put a hurt on the second quarter. I slid into a front seat and waited for the movie to start.

*Panic in the Year Zero* is not as I thought at the time science fiction in that the only thing that would make it so is the portrayals of atomic bombs going off. Something that was all too possible at the time and sadly still much too likely today. The story starts with a normal family – one father, one mother, one teenage son, a younger teenage daughter. The father, middle class average Joe, the mother, a stay-at-home housewife, the teenage son in that area where he's still got a lot of kid in him but can see manhood ahead and longs to get there, the daughter at the stay in my room and adults are dumb and this trip is boring. Just an average family heading on vacation, driving from their home in a suburb of Los Angeles to a quiet country lake vacation spot like millions of people do every vacation. Until there is a flash of intense light behind them; not lightning, more like the world's largest flashbulb going off. The normal every day family are now survivors of an atomic attack on the United States. They aren't preppers, so how do they manage to make it through to a new civilization after the attack? That's the question the movie answers for us.

After the movie is over, I head out to cross the street to check out Stove's newsstand. Stove's is more than a place to buy the newspapers from all across the country; it's also a bookstore- get the latest paperbacks here – a comic book shop – best sellers Batman and Superman, there are no Marvel heroes yet. I picked out one of the current issues, handed over my last dime and headed back to the Taxi company office. Stove's becomes important to this a week or two later when I went back and was browsing in the paperback area. There on a shelf was a new book. *The Day the World Ended.* If you haven't guessed already, it was the novelization of the movie. Of course, it told the same story with a few minor changes or additions but turned out to be a good read.

Neither the movie or the book are masterpieces in their genre. But both do tell a good story and they give some hints for preppers as well. Though there were no preppers in 1962 just the average family with a flashlight, household tools, maybe some camping gear especially if the dad was a hunter or the son/daughter was a Boy/Girl Scout and likely a gun of some sort in the house in the south or west or if the dad was a vet of WWII or Korea. The closest person to a prepper as we know them now was the odd family that had a fallout shelter – few and far between.

Let's move on to 1964. It's now the United States after the Cuban missile crisis. There were more families that have fallout shelters but they were still rare. The author of the next book was one of the people that built a shelter and that and the world situation inspired him to write our next survival adventure.

The author is Robert A. Heinlein so you can be fairly sure the book will be a good read. It is but some of the intimate personal relationships and the handling of race are not as well done as they could have been. In a slight defense of it, Heinlein was born in 1907, raised in Missouri, left there to attend the Naval Academy, served aboard U.S. vessels, spent way too much time in Navy Hospitals, all of which were very conservative places and organizations then. He moved to California where he was exposed to a very different type world. Years before he wrote this novel had had written novels where the main heroes in the books were non-white. One was Puerta Rican and the other was black. But, back to the main reason *Farnham's Freehold* is on this list.

Hugh Farnham is a middle-aged man at home with his wife. Coming to dinner is his adult son and his daughter home from college, who had brought a friend with her. They have a nice dinner prepared by their houseboy after which they settle down to play bridge. In the middle of their game the world goes to hell. WWIII has started. Hugh leads everyone downstairs to the shelter he had built. They attempt to continue the bridge session but soon the first bomb hits. Time passes and there are a few more hits until-wham- the biggest hit of all. They survive and finally come out of the shelter and find what looks to be pristine forest.

Now it's time to take care of permanent survival. Hugh has made preparations for this possibility as well as for living through the first hours. The group comes together to build a home out of a wilderness. In the book Hugh has a library of books in the shelter for using to survive and to rebuild civilization.

*Farnham's Freehold* first appeared in print in the science fiction magazine *Worlds of If* running in the July, August, and October issues, with Putnam publishing the print hardback just after that. One of the things I liked when I first read it was that Hugh has a section in one chapter where he thinks of the books he has saved. It was the first time any well-known person had put down a prepper list and it holds up even now. I'll quote the list to you in Hugh's words as written by Heinlein from the book:

> "Someone had put the books back on shelves but some were open to dry; he fluffed these, hoped for the best.
> "The last books in the world--so it seemed. He felt sudden grief that abstract knowledge of deaths of millions had not given him. Somehow, the burning of millions of books felt more brutally obscene than the killing of people. All men must die, it was their single common heritage. But a book need never die and should not be killed; books were the immortal part of man. Book burners-to rape a defenseless friendly book. Books had always been his best friends. In a hundred public libraries they had taught him. From a thousand newsstands they had warmed his loneliness. He suddenly felt that if he had not been able to save some books, it would hardly be worthwhile to live. Most of his collection was functional: The Encyclopedia Britannica ... He had grudged its bulkiness, too, but it was the most compact assemblage of knowledge on the market. "Che" Guevera's *War of the Guerillas*-thank God he wasn't going to need that! Nor those next to it: "Yank" Leivy's manual on resistance fighting, Griffith's *Translation of Mao Tse-tungs On Guerilla Warfare,* Tom Wintringham's *New Ways of War,* the new TR on special operations-forget

'em! Ain't a-gonna study war no more! The *Boy Scout Handbook, Eshbach's Mechanical Engineering, The Radio Repairman's Guide, Outdoor Life's Hunting and Fishing, Edible Fungi and How to Know Them, Home Life in the Colonial Days, Your Log Cabin, Chimneys and Fireplaces, The Hobo's Cook Book, Medicine Without a Doctor, Five Acres and Independence, Russian Self-Taught* and English-Russian and Russian-English dictionaries, *The Complete Herbalist*, the survival manuals of the Navy Bureau of Weapons, *The Air Force's Survival Techniques, The Practical Carpenter*-all sound books, of the brown and useful sort. *The Oxford Book of English Verse, A Treasury of American Poetry, Hoyle's Book of Games, Burton's Anatomy of Melancholy,* a different Burton's *Thousand Nights and a Night*, the good old *Odyssey* with the Wyeth illustrations, Kipling's *Collected Verse*, and his *Just So Stories*, a one-volume Shakespeare, the *Book of Common Prayer*, the *Bible, Mathematical Recreations and Essays, Thus Spake Zarathustra*, T. S. Eliot's *The Old Possum's Book of Practical Cats,* Robert Frost's Verse, *Men Against the Sea*--He wished that he had found time to stock the list of fiction he had started. He wished that he had fetched down his works of Mark Twain regardless of space. He wished—Too late, too late. This was it. All that was left of a mighty civilization."

I have my own list, some are on Heinlein's list and some are not. I do have one advantage that was not available when the 1964 list was made. I have an e-reader that has space for hundreds of books and a solar charger, both of which will last for years, I also have hard copies of many books I'd want to have as well. We'll truck on to more modern times now.

One of the things that could cause great damage to civilization is an EMP event. EMP – electro-magnetic pulse- can be caused by exploding a nuclear weapon high in the atmosphere or by a massive solar flare from the sun that hits the earth. First example – The United States did a high-altitude nuclear bomb test in 1962 in the middle of the Pacific Ocean called Starfish Prime. It caused an electromagnetic pulse (EMP) that knocked out streetlights and damaged electronics in Hawaii over 900 miles from the test. Second example – in 1859 there was a massive solar flare now called the Carrington Event. It caused the auroras to be seen as far south as the tropics, and significant disruption to telegraph systems, with operators reporting sparks, shocks, and even fires.

Our fiction event occurs most likely (using the publication date and clues in the book) in 2009 at 4:50 p.m. (16:50) Eastern Daylight Time on the second Tuesday of May. We find out that high-altitude nuclear explosions have happened over the US and Europe, and Russia. The world just dropped back to using the technical knowledge of the mid-1800s. The story tells of the ways the hero of the book, his family, and his friends and fellow residents of the small valley in Black Mountain, North Carolina manage to make new lives with what they have and know. The single book would turn into a series. Good reading for preppers. Here are the books: *One Second After, One Year After, Five Years After*, and *The Final Day*. I'll leave this at that point so you can find the books to enjoy reading them yourselves.

I would now like to take us to the far future. I'm going back to Heinlein again. This is a world where science has found a way to open a portal to another world; a tunnel from here to there if you will. Or as the title puts it, *Tunnel in the Sky*. The hero of the book is Rod Walker, a high school senior about to take his final exam in a class he needs to accomplish his goal of going off world. The book opens with him reading a notice about the final exam:

"PATRICK HENRY HIGH SCHOOL
Department of Social Studies
SPECIAL NOTICE to all students Course 410
(elective senior seminar) Advanced Survival,
instr. Dr. Matson, 1712-A MWF

1. There will be no class Friday the 14th.

2. Twenty-Four Hour Notice is hereby given of final examination in Solo Survival. Students will present themselves for physical check at 0900 Saturday in the dispensary of Templeton Gate and will start passing through the gate at 1000, using three-minute intervals by lot.

3. TEST CONDITIONS:

(a) ANY planet, ANY climate, ANY terrain;

(b) NO rules, ALL weapons, ANY equipment;

(c) TEAMING IS PERMITTED but teams will not be allowed to pass through the gate in company;

(d) TEST DURATION is not less than forty-eight hours, not more than ten days.

4. Dr. Matson will be available for advice and consultation until 1700 Friday.

5. Test may be postponed Only on recommendation of examining physician, but any student may withdraw from the course without administrative penalty up until 1000 Saturday.

6. Good luck and long life to you all!

(s) B. P. Matson, Sc.D.

Approved:

J. R. ROERICH, for the Board"

He will take the exam but one small problem; there is a nova on a nearby star system and suddenly the tunnel is gone and likely to stay gone for years or forever. This one is a good one, but it is a coming-of-age story. It is also one of Heinlein's juvenal novels. It still remains a story worth reading. There are a goodly number of hints a person could use in a survival situation. It will make you think if you are planning on living through -pick your own worst-case scenario. If you want to find out how well you would, here's a challenge for you:

1. Pick what you think you will need for a 48-hour period. Only one small snack is allowed.
2. Have a friend pick a place within (a state park, national park or ask someone that has a large acre of land you can use) four hours of your home.
3. Pick a long weekend either in the late spring or early fall.
4. Have the friend blindfold you, then drive you to a spot they have chosen on the land. Have him take a long route to the place, maybe drive in a circle a few times to get you out of figuring out where you are.
5. Have him shake your hand and drive off.

6. Now survive. Get picked up 48 hours after you were dropped off.
7. If this is no big deal for you, repeat at a later time running it for a week.

This is for those that think you can play the lone wolf should a doomsday event ever occur. I refer you to the first Kipling poem I put in the chapter on poetry. Good Luck and I'll see you on the day after doomsday.

# Shall We Sit and Talk a Little Treason

This one's full of sedition, conspiracy, and dare I say it treason.

This chapter I bring you firebrands with ideas such as these:

"All people are equal, they have specific rights, such as existence, autonomy and to seek contentment; governments are made by men to safeguard these privileges, and from the people they receive their powers, —It is also held that when any government becomes threaten or remove these rights, it is appropriate that the people to correct or to eradicate it, and to found a new government, determining a form that will most likely insure the right they must maintain this should not be done lightly but when a long history of exploitations and usurpations, shows a tend to render the people under that government to a condition of absolute despotism, it is the people's right, their duty, to over throw such a government, and to establish a new form of government to provide for their future security."

"But the most powerful of all arguments, is, that nothing but independence, i.e. a new form of government, can keep the peace of the land and preserve it inviolate from civil wars."

"A government of our own is the people's natural right."

"[We] see that bribery, corruption, and favouritism are the standing vices of governments."

"The property of no man is secure in the present unsupported system of things."

"Those who would give up essential Liberty, to purchase a little temporary Safety, deserve neither Liberty nor Safety."

"It is the first responsibility of every citizen to question authority."

"Without freedom of thought, there can be no such thing as wisdom; and no such thing as public liberty without freedom of speech; which is the right of every man as far as by it he does not hurt or control the right of another; and this is the only check it ought to suffer and the only bounds it ought to know.... Whoever would overthrow the liberty of a nation must begin by subduing the freedom of speech, a thing terrible to traitors."

At this point I must tell you the names of the three men that made the above quotes though I must state that in the first five I have updated the wording to current usage and somewhat modified the quote for clearer meaning in this time while the last three are direct and complete as they were first made. I have hopes that by this point most all of my readers have recognized the words if not the authors of them.

The first long list is from Thomas Jefferson, the next five are from Thomas Paine, and the last two by Benjamin Franklin.

You may ask why these men and their writings appear in this chapter of forgotten and dusty books. The answer is a simple one. I taught history and had hopes of passing on some of the wisdom and thinking of the great men of United States history. I don't know if overall I had a great deal of success in this hope; yes, my students passed their tests, but you never know if anything sticks with them past their finishing of the tests. There was an experiment done in New York City where people were stopped and some of the quotes I used above were read to them. They were asked their thoughts on the quotes. A very small percentage recognized them for what they are but most had no idea where they came from and a large percentage thought they were from subversive groups against the government.

Good reader, if you haven't read the Declaration of Independence since you were in middle or high school or even read the full text of Paine's *Common Sense* both are online and easy to find. Search out a copy of them and read them to understand the founding principles of our country.

As for Doctor Franklin and his quotes you can't go wrong reading him. He has a ready wit that comes through his works and can bring a smile or chuckle with his comments. He also cuts to the quick of the matter and readily shares his insights with you.

I'll leave you with a Franklin story. Doctor Franklin was departing the hall where the new government of the United States was being consolidated. He was approached on the street by a lady who spoke to him and said, "Well, Doctor Franklin, what form of government do we have?"

"We have given you a republic, madam, if you can keep it," was his reply.

A republic if you can keep it. Words to bear in mind then and now.

Reader, I decided to save you time. Here are the full texts of the two documents that all Americans should know and protect. In fact, I took an oath many years ago swearing to protect and defend the Constitution of the United States. The oath still holds for me and a lot of others that took the oath. Here are the Declaration of Independence and The Constitution of the United States. I ask that you read and contemplate the meanings and ideals that they represent.

# In Congress, July 4, 1776

**The unanimous Declaration of the thirteen united States of America,** When in the Course of human events, it becomes necessary for one people to dissolve the political bands which have connected them with another, and to assume among the powers of the earth, the separate and equal station to which the Laws of Nature and of Nature's God entitle them, a decent respect to the opinions of mankind requires that they should declare the causes which impel them to the separation.

We hold these truths to be self-evident, that all men are created equal, that they are endowed by their Creator with certain unalienable Rights, that among these are Life, Liberty and the pursuit of Happiness.--That to secure these rights, Governments are instituted among Men, deriving their just powers from the consent of the governed, --That whenever any Form of Government becomes destructive of these ends, it is the Right of the People to alter or to abolish it, and to institute new Government, laying its foundation on such principles and organizing its powers in such form, as to them shall seem most likely to affect their Safety and Happiness. Prudence, indeed, will dictate that Governments long established should not be changed for light and transient causes; and accordingly, all experience hath shewn, that mankind are more disposed to suffer, while evils are sufferable, than to right themselves by abolishing the forms to which they are accustomed. But when a long train of abuses and usurpations, pursuing invariably the same Object evinces a design to reduce them under absolute Despotism, it is their right, it is their duty, to throw off such Government, and to provide new Guards for their future security.--Such has been the patient sufferance of these Colonies; and such is now the necessity which constrains them to alter their former Systems of Government. The history of the present King of Great Britain is a history of repeated injuries and usurpations, all having in direct object the establishment of an absolute Tyranny over these States. To prove this, let Facts be submitted to a candid world.

He has refused his Assent to Laws, the most wholesome and necessary for the public good.

He has forbidden his Governors to pass Laws of immediate and pressing importance, unless suspended in their operation till his Assent should be obtained; and when so suspended, he has utterly neglected to attend to them.

He has refused to pass other Laws for the accommodation of large districts of people, unless those people would relinquish the right of Representation in the Legislature, a right inestimable to them and formidable to tyrants only.

He has called together legislative bodies at places unusual, uncomfortable, and distant from the depository of their public Records, for the sole purpose of fatiguing them into compliance with his measures.

He has dissolved Representative Houses repeatedly, for opposing with manly firmness his invasions on the rights of the people.

He has refused for a long time, after such dissolutions, to cause others to be elected; whereby the Legislative powers, incapable of Annihilation, have returned to the People at large for their exercise; the State remaining in the mean time exposed to all the dangers of invasion from without, and convulsions within.

He has endeavoured to prevent the population of these States; for that purpose obstructing the Laws for Naturalization of Foreigners; refusing to pass others to encourage their migrations hither, and raising the conditions of new Appropriations of Lands.

He has obstructed the Administration of Justice, by refusing his Assent to Laws for establishing Judiciary powers.
He has made Judges dependent on his Will alone, for the tenure of their offices, and the amount and payment of their salaries.

He has erected a multitude of New Offices, and sent hither swarms of Officers to harrass our people, and eat out their substance.

He has kept among us, in times of peace, Standing Armies without the Consent of our legislatures.

He has affected to render the Military independent of and superior to the Civil power.

He has combined with others to subject us to a jurisdiction foreign to our constitution, and unacknowledged by our laws; giving his Assent to their Acts of pretended Legislation:

For Quartering large bodies of armed troops among us:

For protecting them, by a mock Trial, from punishment for any Murders which they should commit on the Inhabitants of these States:

For cutting off our Trade with all parts of the world:

For imposing Taxes on us without our Consent:

For depriving us in many cases, of the benefits of Trial by Jury:

For transporting us beyond Seas to be tried for pretended offences:

For abolishing the free System of English Laws in a neighbouring Province, establishing therein an Arbitrary government, and enlarging its Boundaries so as to render it at once an example and fit instrument for introducing the same absolute rule into these Colonies:

For taking away our Charters, abolishing our most valuable Laws, and altering fundamentally the Forms of our Governments:

For suspending our own Legislatures, and declaring themselves invested with power to legislate for us in all cases whatsoever.

He has abdicated Government here, by declaring us out of his Protection and waging War against us.

He has plundered our seas, ravaged our Coasts, burnt our towns, and destroyed the lives of our people.

He is at this time transporting large Armies of foreign Mercenaries to compleat the works of death, desolation and tyranny, already begun with circumstances of Cruelty & perfidy scarcely paralleled in the most barbarous ages, and totally unworthy the Head of a civilized nation.

He has constrained our fellow Citizens taken Captive on the high Seas to bear Arms against their Country, to become the executioners of their friends and Brethren, or to fall themselves by their Hands.

He has excited domestic insurrections amongst us, and has endeavoured to bring on the inhabitants of our frontiers, the merciless Indian Savages, whose known rule of warfare, is an undistinguished destruction of all ages, sexes and conditions.

In every stage of these Oppressions We have Petitioned for Redress in the most humble terms: Our repeated Petitions have been answered only by repeated injury. A Prince, whose character is thus marked by every act which may define a Tyrant, is unfit to be the ruler of a free people.

Nor have We been wanting in attentions to our British brethren. We have warned them from time to time of attempts by their legislature to extend an unwarrantable jurisdiction over us. We have reminded them of the circumstances of our emigration and settlement here. We have appealed to their native justice and magnanimity, and we have conjured them by the ties of our common kindred to disavow these usurpations, which, would inevitably interrupt our connections and correspondence. They too have been deaf to the voice of justice and of consanguinity. We must, therefore, acquiesce in the necessity, which denounces our Separation, and hold them, as we hold the rest of mankind, Enemies in War, in Peace Friends.

We, therefore, the Representatives of the United States of America, in General Congress, Assembled, appealing to the Supreme Judge of the world for the rectitude of our intentions, do, in the Name, and by Authority of the good People of these Colonies, solemnly publish and declare, That these United Colonies are, and of Right ought to be Free and Independent States; that they are Absolved from all Allegiance to the British Crown, and that all political connection between them and the State of Great Britain, is and ought to be totally dissolved; and that as Free and Independent States, they have full Power to levy War, conclude Peace, contract Alliances, establish Commerce, and to do all other Acts and Things which Independent States may of right do. And for the support of this Declaration, with a firm reliance on the protection of divine Providence, we mutually pledge to each other our Lives, our Fortunes and our sacred Honor.

**Georgia**
Button Gwinnett
Lyman Hall
George Walton

**Maryland**
Samuel Chase
William Pica
Thomas Stone
Charles Carroll of
 Carrollton

**Delaware**
Caesar Rodney
George Read

Thomas McKean

**Massachusetts**
Samuel Adams
John Adams
Robert Treat Paine
Elbridge Gerry

**North Carolina**
William Hooper
Joseph Hewes
John Penn

**Virginia**
George Wythe

Richard Henry Lee
Thomas Jefferson
Benjamin Harrison
Thomas Nelson, Jr.
Francis Lightfoot Lee
Carter Braxton

**New York**
William Floyd
Philip Livingston
Francis Lewis
Lewis Morris

**Rhode Island**
Stephen Hopkins
Willian Ellery

**South Carolina**
Edward Rutledge
Thomas Lynch, Jr.
Thomas Heward, Jr.
Arthur Middleton

**New Hampshire**
Josiah Barlett
William Whipple

Matthew Thornton

**Pennsylvania**
Robert Morris
Benjamin Rush
Benjamin Franklin
John Morton
George Clymer
James Smith
George Taylor
James Wilson
George Ross

**Connecticut**
Roger Sherman
Samuel Huntington
William Williams
Oliver Wolcott

**New Jersey**
Richard Stockton
John Witherspoon
John Hart
Abraham Clark
Francis Hopkinson

**Massachusetts**
# John Hancock

# Constitution of the United States

**We the People** of the United States, in Order to form a more perfect Union, establish Justice, insure domestic Tranquility, provide for the common defence, promote the general Welfare, and secure the Blessings of Liberty to ourselves and our Posterity, do ordain and establish this Constitution for the United States of America.

**Article I**
**Section 1**
All legislative Powers herein granted shall be vested in a Congress of the United States, which shall consist of a Senate and House of Representatives.

**Section 2**
The House of Representatives shall be composed of Members chosen every second Year by the People of the several States, and the Electors in each State shall have the Qualifications requisite for Electors of the most numerous Branch of the State Legislature.

No Person shall be a Representative who shall not have attained to the Age of twenty-five Years, and been seven Years a Citizen of the United States, and who shall not, when elected, be an Inhabitant of that State in which he shall be chosen.

Representatives and direct Taxes shall be apportioned among the several States which may be included within this Union, according to their respective Numbers, which shall be determined by adding to the whole Number of free Persons, including those bound to Service for a Term of Years, and excluding Indians not taxed, three fifths of all other Persons. The actual Enumeration shall be made within three Years after the first Meeting of the Congress of the United States, and within every subsequent Term of ten Years, in such Manner as they shall by Law direct. The Number of Representatives shall not exceed one for every thirty Thousand, but each State shall have at Least one Representative; and until such enumeration shall be made, the State of New Hampshire shall be entitled to chuse three, Massachusetts eight,

Rhode Island and Providence Plantations one, Connecticut five, New-York six, New Jersey four, Pennsylvania eight, Delaware one, Maryland six, Virginia ten, North Carolina five, South Carolina five, and Georgia three.

When vacancies happen in the Representation from any State, the Executive Authority thereof shall issue Writs of Election to fill such Vacancies.

The House of Representatives shall chuse their Speaker and other Officers; and shall have the sole Power of Impeachment.

**Section 3**

The Senate of the United States shall be composed of two Senators from each State, chosen by the Legislature thereof, for six Years; and each Senator shall have one Vote.

Immediately after they shall be assembled in Consequence of the first Election, they shall be divided as equally as may be into three Classes. The Seats of the Senators of the first Class shall be vacated at the Expiration of the second Year, of the second Class at the Expiration of the fourth Year, and of the third Class at the Expiration of the sixth Year, so that one third may be chosen every second Year; and if Vacancies happen by Resignation, or otherwise, during the Recess of the Legislature of any State, the Executive thereof may make temporary Appointments until the next Meeting of the Legislature, which shall then fill such Vacancies.

No Person shall be a Senator who shall not have attained to the Age of thirty Years, and been nine Years a Citizen of the United States, and who shall not, when elected, be an Inhabitant of that State for which he shall be chosen.

The Vice President of the United States shall be President of the Senate, but shall have no Vote, unless they be equally divided.

The Senate shall chuse their other Officers, and also a President pro tempore, in the Absence of the Vice President, or when he shall exercise the Office of President of the United States.

The Senate shall have the sole Power to try all Impeachments. When sitting for that Purpose, they shall be on Oath or Affirmation. When the President of the United States is tried, the

Chief Justice shall preside: And no Person shall be convicted without the Concurrence of two thirds of the Members present.

Judgment in Cases of Impeachment shall not extend further than to removal from Office, and disqualification to hold and enjoy any Office of honor, Trust or Profit under the United States: but the Party convicted shall nevertheless be liable and subject to Indictment, Trial, Judgment and Punishment, according to Law.

**Section 4**

The Times, Places and Manner of holding Elections for Senators and Representatives, shall be prescribed in each State by the Legislature thereof; but the Congress may at any time by Law make or alter such Regulations, except as to the Places of chusing Senators.

The Congress shall assemble at least once in every Year, and such Meeting shall be on the first Monday in December, unless they shall by Law appoint a different Day.

**Section 5**

Each House shall be the Judge of the Elections, Returns and Qualifications of its own Members, and a Majority of each shall constitute a Quorum to do Business; but a smaller Number may adjourn from day to day, and may be authorized to compel the Attendance of absent Members, in such Manner, and under such Penalties as each House may provide.

Each House may determine the Rules of its Proceedings, punish its Members for disorderly Behaviour, and, with the Concurrence of two thirds, expel a Member.

Each House shall keep a Journal of its Proceedings, and from time to time publish the same, excepting such Parts as may in their Judgment require Secrecy; and the Yeas and Nays of the Members of either House on any question shall, at the Desire of one fifth of those Present, be entered on the Journal.

Neither House, during the Session of Congress, shall, without the Consent of the other, adjourn for more than three days, nor to any other Place than that in which the two Houses shall be sitting.

## Section 6

The Senators and Representatives shall receive a Compensation for their Services, to be ascertained by Law, and paid out of the Treasury of the United States. They shall in all Cases, except Treason, Felony and Breach of the Peace, be privileged from Arrest during their Attendance at the Session of their respective Houses, and in going to and returning from the same; and for any Speech or Debate in either House, they shall not be questioned in any other Place.

No Senator or Representative shall, during the Time for which he was elected, be appointed to any civil Office under the Authority of the United States, which shall have been created, or the Emoluments whereof shall have been encreased during such time; and no Person holding any Office under the United States, shall be a Member of either House during his Continuance in Office.

## Section 7

All Bills for raising Revenue shall originate in the House of Representatives; but the Senate may propose or concur with Amendments as on other Bills.

Every Bill which shall have passed the House of Representatives and the Senate, shall, before it become a Law, be presented to the President of the United States; If he approve he shall sign it, but if not he shall return it, with his Objections to that House in which it shall have originated, who shall enter the Objections at large on their Journal, and proceed to reconsider it. If after such Reconsideration two thirds of that House shall agree to pass the Bill, it shall be sent, together with the Objections, to the other House, by which it shall likewise be reconsidered, and if approved by two thirds of that House, it shall become a Law. But in all such Cases the Votes of both Houses shall be determined by yeas and Nays, and the Names of the Persons voting for and against the Bill shall be entered on the Journal of each House respectively. If any Bill shall not be returned by the President within ten Days (Sundays excepted) after it shall have been presented to him, the Same shall be a Law, in like Manner as if he had signed it, unless the Congress by their Adjournment prevent its Return, in which Case it shall not be a Law.

Every Order, Resolution, or Vote to which the Concurrence of the Senate and House of Representatives may be necessary (except on a question of Adjournment) shall be presented to the President of the United States; and before the Same shall take Effect, shall be approved by him, or being disapproved by him, shall be repassed by two thirds of the Senate and House of Representatives, according to the Rules and Limitations prescribed in the Case of a Bill.

**Section 8**

The Congress shall have Power To lay and collect Taxes, Duties, Imposts and Excises, to pay the Debts and provide for the common Defence and general Welfare of the United States; but all Duties, Imposts and Excises shall be uniform throughout the United States;

To borrow Money on the credit of the United States;

To regulate Commerce with foreign Nations, and among the several States, and with the Indian Tribes;

To establish an uniform Rule of Naturalization, and uniform Laws on the subject of Bankruptcies throughout the United States;

To coin Money, regulate the Value thereof, and of foreign Coin, and fix the Standard of Weights and Measures;

To provide for the Punishment of counterfeiting the Securities and current Coin of the United States;

To establish Post Offices and post Roads;

To promote the Progress of Science and useful Arts, by securing for limited Times to Authors and Inventors the exclusive Right to their respective Writings and Discoveries;

To constitute Tribunals inferior to the supreme Court;

To define and punish Piracies and Felonies committed on the high Seas, and Offences against the Law of Nations;

To declare War, grant Letters of Marque and Reprisal, and make Rules concerning Captures on Land and Water;

To raise and support Armies, but no Appropriation of Money to that Use shall be for a longer Term than two Years;

To provide and maintain a Navy;

To make Rules for the Government and Regulation of the land and naval Forces;

To provide for calling forth the Militia to execute the Laws of the Union, suppress Insurrections and repel Invasions;

To provide for organizing, arming, and disciplining, the Militia, and for governing such Part of them as may be employed in the Service of the United States, reserving to the States respectively, the Appointment of the Officers, and the Authority of training the Militia according to the discipline prescribed by Congress;

To exercise exclusive Legislation in all Cases whatsoever, over such District (not exceeding ten Miles square) as may, by Cession of particular States, and the Acceptance of Congress, become the Seat of Government of the United States, and to exercise like Authority over all Places purchased by the Consent of the Legislature of the State in which the Same shall be, for the Erection of Forts, Magazines, Arsenals, dock-Yards, and other needful Buildings;–And

To make all Laws which shall be necessary and proper for carrying into Execution the foregoing Powers, and all other Powers vested by this Constitution in the Government of the United States, or in any Department or Officer thereof.

**Section 9**

The Migration or Importation of such Persons as any of the States now existing shall think proper to admit, shall not be prohibited by the Congress prior to the Year one thousand eight hundred and eight, but a Tax or duty may be imposed on such Importation, not exceeding ten dollars for each Person.

The Privilege of the Writ of Habeas Corpus shall not be suspended, unless when in Cases of Rebellion or Invasion the public Safety may require it.

No Bill of Attainder or ex post facto Law shall be passed.

No Capitation, or other direct, Tax shall be laid, unless in Proportion to the Census or enumeration herein before directed to be taken.

No Tax or Duty shall be laid on Articles exported from any State.

No Preference shall be given by any Regulation of Commerce or Revenue to the Ports of one State over those of another: nor shall Vessels bound to, or from, one State, be obliged to enter, clear, or pay Duties in another.

No Money shall be drawn from the Treasury, but in Consequence of Appropriations made by Law; and a regular Statement and Account of the Receipts and Expenditures of all public Money shall be published from time to time.

No Title of Nobility shall be granted by the United States: And no Person holding any Office of Profit or Trust under them, shall, without the Consent of the Congress, accept of any present, Emolument, Office, or Title, of any kind whatever, from any King, Prince, or foreign State.

**Section 10**
No State shall enter into any Treaty, Alliance, or Confederation; grant Letters of Marque and Reprisal; coin Money; emit Bills of Credit; make any Thing but gold and silver Coin a Tender in Payment of Debts; pass any Bill of Attainder, ex post facto Law, or Law impairing the Obligation of Contracts, or grant any Title of Nobility.

No State shall, without the Consent of the Congress, lay any Imposts or Duties on Imports or Exports, except what may be absolutely necessary for executing it's inspection Laws: and the net Produce of all Duties and Imposts, laid by any State on Imports or Exports, shall be for the Use of the Treasury of the United States; and all such Laws shall be subject to the Revision and Controul of the Congress.

No State shall, without the Consent of Congress, lay any Duty of Tonnage, keep Troops, or Ships of War in time of Peace, enter into any Agreement or Compact with another State, or with a foreign Power, or engage in War, unless actually invaded, or in such imminent Danger as will not admit of delay.

**Article II**
**Section 1**
The executive Power shall be vested in a President of the United States of America. He shall hold his Office during the Term of four

Years, and, together with the Vice President, chosen for the same Term, be elected, as follows

Each State shall appoint, in such Manner as the Legislature thereof may direct, a Number of Electors, equal to the whole Number of Senators and Representatives to which the State may be entitled in the Congress: but no Senator or Representative, or Person holding an Office of Trust or Profit under the United States, shall be appointed an Elector.

The Electors shall meet in their respective States, and vote by Ballot for two Persons, of whom one at least shall not be an Inhabitant of the same State with themselves. And they shall make a List of all the Persons voted for, and of the Number of Votes for each; which List they shall sign and certify, and transmit sealed to the Seat of the Government of the United States, directed to the President of the Senate. The President of the Senate shall, in the Presence of the Senate and House of Representatives, open all the Certificates, and the Votes shall then be counted. The Person having the greatest Number of Votes shall be the President, if such Number be a Majority of the whole Number of Electors appointed; and if there be more than one who have such Majority, and have an equal Number of Votes, then the House of Representatives shall immediately chuse by Ballot one of them for President; and if no Person have a Majority, then from the five highest on the List the said House shall in like Manner chuse the President. But in chusing the President, the Votes shall be taken by States, the Representation from each State having one Vote; A quorum for this Purpose shall consist of a Member or Members from two thirds of the States, and a Majority of all the States shall be necessary to a Choice. In every Case, after the Choice of the President, the Person having the greatest Number of Votes of the Electors shall be the Vice President. But if there should remain two or more who have equal Votes, the Senate shall chuse from them by Ballot the Vice President.

The Congress may determine the Time of chusing the Electors, and the Day on which they shall give their Votes; which Day shall be the same throughout the United States.

No Person except a natural born Citizen, or a Citizen of the

United States, at the time of the Adoption of this Constitution, shall be eligible to the Office of President; neither shall any Person be eligible to that Office who shall not have attained to the Age of thirty five Years, and been fourteen Years a Resident within the United States.

In Case of the Removal of the President from Office, or of his Death, Resignation, or Inability to discharge the Powers and Duties of the said Office, the Same shall devolve on the Vice President, and the Congress may by law provide for the Case of Removal, Death, Resignation or Inability, both of the President and Vice President, declaring what Officer shall then act as President, and such Officer shall act accordingly, until the Disability be removed, or a President shall be elected.

The President shall, at stated Times, receive for his Services, a Compensation, which shall neither be encreased nor diminished during the Period for which he shall have been elected, and he shall not receive within that Period any other Emolument from the United States, or any of them.

Before he enter on the Execution of his Office, he shall take the following Oath or Affirmation:– I do solemnly swear (or affirm) that I will faithfully execute the Office of President of the United States, and will to the best of my Ability, preserve, protect and defend the Constitution of the United States.

**Section 2**

The President shall be Commander in Chief of the Army and Navy of the United States, and of the Militia of the several States, when called into the actual Service of the United States; he may require the Opinion, in writing, of the principal Officer in each of the executive Departments, upon any Subject relating to the Duties of their respective Offices, and he shall have Power to grant Reprieves and Pardons for Offences against the United States, except in Cases of Impeachment.

He shall have Power, by and with the Advice and Consent of the Senate, to make Treaties, provided two thirds of the Senators present concur; and he shall nominate, and by and with the Advice and Consent of the Senate, shall appoint Ambassadors, other public Ministers and Consuls, Judges of the supreme Court, and all other Officers of the United States, whose Appointments are not herein otherwise provided for, and which shall be established by Law: but the Congress may by Law vest the Appointment of such inferior Officers, as they think proper, in the President alone, in the Courts of Law, or in the Heads of Departments.

The President shall have Power to fill up all Vacancies that may happen during the Recess of the Senate, by granting Commissions which shall expire at the End of their next Session.

**Section 3**

He shall from time to time give to the Congress Information of the State of the Union, and recommend to their Consideration such Measures as he shall judge necessary and expedient; he may, on extraordinary Occasions, convene both Houses, or either of them, and in Case of Disagreement between them, with Respect to the Time of Adjournment, he may adjourn them to such Time as he shall think proper; he shall receive Ambassadors and other public Ministers; he shall take Care that the Laws be faithfully executed, and shall Commission all the Officers of the United States.

**Section 4**

The President, Vice President and all civil Officers of the United States, shall be removed from Office on Impeachment for, and Conviction of, Treason, Bribery, or other high Crimes and Misdemeanors.

**Article III**
**Section 1**

The judicial Power of the United States, shall be vested in one supreme Court, and in such inferior Courts as the Congress may from time to time ordain and establish. The Judges, both of the supreme and inferior Courts, shall hold their Offices during good Behaviour, and shall, at stated Times, receive for their Services, a Compensation, which shall not be diminished during their Continuance in Office.

**Section 2**

The judicial Power shall extend to all Cases, in Law and Equity, arising under this Constitution, the Laws of the United States, and Treaties made, or which shall be made, under their Authority;—to all Cases affecting Ambassadors, other public Ministers and Consuls;—to all Cases of admiralty and maritime Jurisdiction;—to Controversies to which the United States shall be a Party;—to Controversies between two or more States;—between a State and Citizens of another State,—between Citizens of different States,—between Citizens of the same State claiming Lands under Grants of different States, and between a State, or the Citizens thereof, and foreign States, Citizens or Subjects.

In all Cases affecting Ambassadors, other public Ministers and Consuls, and those in which a State shall be Party, the supreme Court shall have original Jurisdiction. In all the other Cases before mentioned, the supreme Court shall have appellate Jurisdiction, both as to Law and Fact, with such Exceptions, and under such Regulations as the Congress shall make.

The Trial of all Crimes, except in Cases of Impeachment, shall be by Jury; and such Trial shall be held in the State where the said Crimes shall have been committed; but when not committed within any State, the Trial shall be at such Place or Places as the Congress may by Law have directed.

**Section 3**
Treason against the United States, shall consist only in levying War against them, or in adhering to their Enemies, giving them Aid and Comfort. No Person shall be convicted of Treason unless on the Testimony of two Witnesses to the same overt Act, or on Confession in open Court.

The Congress shall have Power to declare the Punishment of Treason, but no Attainder of Treason shall work Corruption of Blood, or Forfeiture except during the Life of the Person attainted.

**Article IV**
**Section 1**
Full Faith and Credit shall be given in each State to the public Acts, Records, and judicial Proceedings of every other State. And the Congress may by general Laws prescribe the Manner in which such Acts, Records and Proceedings shall be proved, and the Effect

thereof.

**Section 2**

The Citizens of each State shall be entitled to all Privileges and Immunities of Citizens in the several States.

A Person charged in any State with Treason, Felony, or other Crime, who shall flee from Justice, and be found in another State, shall on Demand of the executive Authority of the State from which he fled, be delivered up, to be removed to the State having Jurisdiction of the Crime.

No Person held to Service or Labour in one State, under the Laws thereof, escaping into another, shall, in Consequence of any Law or Regulation therein, be discharged from such Service or Labour, but shall be delivered up on Claim of the Party to whom such Service or Labour may be due.

**Section 3**

New States may be admitted by the Congress into this Union; but no new State shall be formed or erected within the Jurisdiction of any other State; nor any State be formed by the Junction of two or more States, or Parts of States, without the Consent of the Legislatures of the States concerned as well as of the Congress.

The Congress shall have Power to dispose of and make all needful Rules and Regulations respecting the Territory or other Property belonging to the United States; and nothing in this Constitution shall be so construed as to Prejudice any Claims of the United States, or of any particular State.

**Section 4**

The United States shall guarantee to every State in this Union a Republican Form of Government, and shall protect each of them against Invasion; and on Application of the Legislature, or of the Executive (when the Legislature cannot be convened) against domestic Violence.

**Article V**

The Congress, whenever two thirds of both Houses shall deem

it necessary, shall propose Amendments to this Constitution, or, on the Application of the Legislatures of two thirds of the several States, shall call a Convention for proposing Amendments, which, in either Case, shall be valid to all Intents and Purposes, as Part of this Constitution, when ratified by the Legislatures of three fourths of the several States, or by Conventions in three fourths thereof, as the one or the other Mode of Ratification may be proposed by the Congress; Provided that no Amendment which may be made prior to the Year One thousand eight hundred and eight shall in any Manner affect the first and fourth Clauses in the Ninth Section of the first Article; and that no State, without its Consent, shall be deprived of its equal Suffrage in the Senate.

**Article VI**
All Debts contracted and Engagements entered into, before the Adoption of this Constitution, shall be as valid against the United States under this Constitution, as under the Confederation.

This Constitution, and the Laws of the United States which shall be made in Pursuance thereof; and all Treaties made, or which shall be made, under the Authority of the United States, shall be the supreme Law of the Land; and the Judges in every State shall be bound thereby, any Thing in the Constitution or Laws of any State to the Contrary notwithstanding.

The Senators and Representatives before mentioned, and the Members of the several State Legislatures, and all executive and judicial Officers, both of the United States and of the several States, shall be bound by Oath or Affirmation, to support this Constitution; but no religious Test shall ever be required as a Qualification to any Office or public Trust under the United States.

**Article VII**
The Ratification of the Conventions of nine States, shall be sufficient for the Establishment of this Constitution between the States so ratifying the Same.

**First Amendment**
Congress shall make no law respecting an establishment of religion, or prohibiting the free exercise thereof; or abridging the

freedom of speech, or of the press; or the right of the people peaceably to assemble, and to petition the Government for a redress of grievances.

**Second Amendment**

A well regulated Militia, being necessary to the security of a free State, the right of the people to keep and bear Arms, shall not be infringed.

**Third Amendment**

No Soldier shall, in time of peace be quartered in any house, without the consent of the Owner, nor in time of war, but in a manner to be prescribed by law.

**Fourth Amendment**

The right of the people to be secure in their persons, houses, papers, and effects, against unreasonable searches and seizures, shall not be violated, and no Warrants shall issue, but upon probable cause, supported by Oath or affirmation, and particularly describing the place to be searched, and the persons or things to be seized.

**Fifth Amendment**

No person shall be held to answer for a capital, or otherwise infamous crime, unless on a presentment or indictment of a Grand Jury, except in cases arising in the land or naval forces, or in the Militia, when in actual service in time of War or public danger; nor shall any person be subject for the same offence to be twice put in jeopardy of life or limb; nor shall be compelled in any criminal case to be a witness against himself, nor be deprived of life, liberty, or property, without due process of law; nor shall private property be taken for public use, without just compensation.

**Sixth Amendment**

In all criminal prosecutions, the accused shall enjoy the right to a speedy and public trial, by an impartial jury of the State and district wherein the crime shall have been committed, which district shall have been previously ascertained by law, and to be informed of the nature and cause of the accusation; to be confronted with the witnesses against him; to have compulsory process for obtaining witnesses in his favor, and to have the Assistance of Counsel for his defence.

**Seventh Amendment**

In Suits at common law, where the value in controversy shall exceed twenty dollars, the right of trial by jury shall be preserved, and no fact tried by a jury, shall be otherwise re-examined in any Court of the United States, than according to the rules of the common law.

**Eighth Amendment**

Excessive bail shall not be required, nor excessive fines imposed, nor cruel and unusual punishments inflicted.

**Ninth Amendment**

The enumeration in the Constitution, of certain rights, shall not be construed to deny or disparage others retained by the people.

**Tenth Amendment**

The powers not delegated to the United States by the Constitution, nor prohibited by it to the States, are reserved to the States respectively, or to the people.

**Eleventh Amendment**

The Judicial power of the United States shall not be construed to extend to any suit in law or equity, commenced or prosecuted against one of the United States by Citizens of another State, or by Citizens or Subjects of any Foreign State.

**Twelfth Amendment**

The Electors shall meet in their respective states and vote by ballot for President and Vice-President, one of whom, at least, shall not be an inhabitant of the same state with themselves; they shall name in their ballots the person voted for as President, and in distinct ballots the person voted for as Vice-President, and they shall make distinct lists of all persons voted for as President, and of all persons voted for as Vice-President, and of the number of votes for each, which lists they shall sign and certify, and transmit sealed to the seat of the government of the United States, directed to the President of the Senate;–the President of the Senate shall, in the presence of the Senate and House of Representatives, open all the certificates and the votes shall then be counted;–The person having the greatest number of votes for President, shall be the President, if such number be a majority of the whole number of Electors appointed; and if no person have such majority, then from the persons having the highest numbers not exceeding three on the list of those voted for as President, the House of Representatives shall choose immediately, by ballot, the President. But in choosing the President, the votes shall be taken by states, the representation from each state having one vote; a quorum for this purpose shall consist of a member or members from two-thirds of the states, and a majority of all the states shall be necessary to a choice. [And if the House of Representatives shall not choose a President whenever the right of choice shall devolve upon them, before the fourth day of March next following, then the Vice-President shall act as President, as in case of the death or other constitutional disability of the President.–]The person having the greatest number of votes as Vice-President, shall be the Vice-President, if such number be a majority of the whole number of Electors appointed, and if no person have a majority, then from the two highest numbers on the list, the Senate shall choose the Vice-President; a quorum for the purpose shall consist of two-thirds of the whole number of Senators, and a majority of the whole number shall be necessary to a choice. But no person constitutionally ineligible to the office of President shall be eligible to that of Vice-President of the United States.

**Thirteenth Amendment**
**Section 1**
Neither slavery nor involuntary servitude, except as a punishment for crime whereof the party shall have been duly convicted, shall exist within the United States, or any place subject

to their jurisdiction.

**Section 2**
Congress shall have power to enforce this article by appropriate legislation.

**Fourteenth Amendment**
**Section 1**
All persons born or naturalized in the United States, and subject to the jurisdiction thereof, are citizens of the United States and of the State wherein they reside. No State shall make or enforce any law which shall abridge the privileges or immunities of citizens of the United States; nor shall any State deprive any person of life, liberty, or property, without due process of law; nor deny to any person within its jurisdiction the equal protection of the laws.

**Section 2**
Representatives shall be apportioned among the several States according to their respective numbers, counting the whole number of persons in each State, excluding Indians not taxed. But when the right to vote at any election for the choice of electors for President and Vice-President of the United States, Representatives in Congress, the Executive and Judicial officers of a State, or the members of the Legislature thereof, is denied to any of the male inhabitants of such State, being twenty-one years of age, and citizens of the United States, or in any way abridged, except for participation in rebellion, or other crime, the basis of representation therein shall be reduced in the proportion which the number of such male citizens shall bear to the whole number of male citizens twenty-one years of age in such State.

**Section 3**
No person shall be a Senator or Representative in Congress, or elector of President and Vice-President, or hold any office, civil or military, under the United States, or under any State, who, having previously taken an oath, as a member of Congress, or as an officer of the United States, or as a member of any State legislature, or as an executive or judicial officer of any State, to support the

Constitution of the United States, shall have engaged in insurrection or rebellion against the same, or given aid or comfort to the enemies thereof. But Congress may by a vote of two-thirds of each House, remove such disability.

**Section 4**
The validity of the public debt of the United States, authorized by law, including debts incurred for payment of pensions and bounties for services in suppressing insurrection or rebellion, shall not be questioned. But neither the United States nor any State shall assume or pay any debt or obligation incurred in aid of insurrection or rebellion against the United States, or any claim for the loss or emancipation of any slave; but all such debts, obligations and claims shall be held illegal and void.

**Section 5**
The Congress shall have power to enforce, by appropriate legislation, the provisions of this article.

**Fifteenth Amendment**
**Section 1**
The right of citizens of the United States to vote shall not be denied or abridged by the United States or by any State on account of race, color, or previous condition of servitude–

**Section 2**
The Congress shall have power to enforce this article by appropriate legislation.

**Sixteenth Amendment**
The Congress shall have power to lay and collect taxes on incomes, from whatever source derived, without apportionment among the several States, and without regard to any census or enumeration.

**Seventeenth Amendment**
The Senate of the United States shall be composed of two

Senators from each State, elected by the people thereof, for six years; and each Senator shall have one vote. The electors in each State shall have the qualifications requisite for electors of the most numerous branch of the State legislatures.

When vacancies happen in the representation of any State in the Senate, the executive authority of such State shall issue writs of election to fill such vacancies: Provided, That the legislature of any State may empower the executive thereof to make temporary appointments until the people fill the vacancies by election as the legislature may direct.

This amendment shall not be so construed as to affect the election or term of any Senator chosen before it becomes valid as part of the Constitution.

**Eighteenth Amendment**
After one year from the ratification of this article the manufacture, sale, or transportation of intoxicating liquors within, the importation thereof into, or the exportation thereof from the United States and all territory subject to the jurisdiction thereof for beverage purposes is hereby prohibited.

The Congress and the several States shall have concurrent power to enforce this article by appropriate legislation.

This article shall be inoperative unless it shall have been ratified as an amendment to the Constitution by the legislatures of the several States, as provided in the Constitution, within seven years from the date of the submission hereof to the States by the Congress.

**Nineteenth Amendment**
The right of citizens of the United States to vote shall not be denied or abridged by the United States or by any State on account of sex.

Congress shall have power to enforce this article by appropriate legislation.

**Twentieth Amendment**
**Section 1**
The terms of the President and the Vice President shall end at

noon on the 20th day of January, and the terms of Senators and Representatives at noon on the 3d day of January, of the years in which such terms would have ended if this article had not been ratified; and the terms of their successors shall then begin.

**Section 2**
The Congress shall assemble at least once in every year, and such meeting shall begin at noon on the 3d day of January, unless they shall by law appoint a different day.

**Section 3**
If, at the time fixed for the beginning of the term of the President, the President elect shall have died, the Vice President elect shall become President. If a President shall not have been chosen before the time fixed for the beginning of his term, or if the President elect shall have failed to qualify, then the Vice President elect shall act as President until a President shall have qualified; and the Congress may by law provide for the case wherein neither a President elect nor a Vice President elect shall have qualified, declaring who shall then act as President, or the manner in which one who is to act shall be selected, and such person shall act accordingly until a President or Vice President shall have qualified.

**Section 4**
The Congress may by law provide for the case of the death of any of the persons from whom the House of Representatives may choose a President whenever the right of choice shall have devolved upon them, and for the case of the death of any of the persons from whom the Senate may choose a Vice President whenever the right of choice shall have devolved upon them.

**Section 5**
Sections 1 and 2 shall take effect on the 15th day of October following the ratification of this article.

**Section 6**

This article shall be inoperative unless it shall have been ratified as an amendment to the Constitution by the legislatures of three-fourths of the several States within seven years from the date of its submission.

## Twenty-First Amendment
### Section 1
The eighteenth article of amendment to the Constitution of the United States is hereby repealed.

### Section 2
The transportation or importation into any State, Territory, or possession of the United States for delivery or use therein of intoxicating liquors, in violation of the laws thereof, is hereby prohibited.

### Section 3
This article shall be inoperative unless it shall have been ratified as an amendment to the Constitution by conventions in the several States, as provided in the Constitution, within seven years from the date of the submission hereof to the States by the Congress.

## Twenty-Second Amendment
### Section 1
No person shall be elected to the office of the President more than twice, and no person who has held the office of President, or acted as President, for more than two years of a term to which some other person was elected President shall be elected to the office of the President more than once. But this Article shall not apply to any person holding the office of President when this Article was proposed by the Congress, and shall not prevent any person who may be holding the office of President, or acting as President, during the term within which this Article becomes operative from holding the office of President or acting as President during the remainder of such term.

### Section 2
This article shall be inoperative unless it shall have been ratified

as an amendment to the Constitution by the legislatures of three-fourths of the several States within seven years from the date of its submission to the States by the Congress.

**Twenty-Third Amendment**
**Section 1**
The District constituting the seat of Government of the United States shall appoint in such manner as the Congress may direct:

A number of electors of President and Vice President equal to the whole number of Senators and Representatives in Congress to which the District would be entitled if it were a State, but in no event more than the least populous State; they shall be in addition to those appointed by the States, but they shall be considered, for the purposes of the election of President and Vice President, to be electors appointed by a State; and they shall meet in the District and perform such duties as provided by the twelfth article of amendment.

**Section 2**
The Congress shall have power to enforce this article by appropriate legislation.

**Twenty-Fourth Amendment**
**Section 1**
The right of citizens of the United States to vote in any primary or other election for President or Vice President, for electors for President or Vice President, or for Senator or Representative in Congress, shall not be denied or abridged by the United States or any State by reason of failure to pay any poll tax or other tax.

**Section 2**
The Congress shall have power to enforce this article by appropriate legislation.

**Twenty-Fifth Amendment**
**Section 1**
In case of the removal of the President from office or of his

death or resignation, the Vice President shall become President.

**Section 2**
Whenever there is a vacancy in the office of the Vice President, the President shall nominate a Vice President who shall take office upon confirmation by a majority vote of both Houses of Congress.

**Section 3**
Whenever the President transmits to the President pro tempore of the Senate and the Speaker of the House of Representatives his written declaration that he is unable to discharge the powers and duties of his office, and until he transmits to them a written declaration to the contrary, such powers and duties shall be discharged by the Vice President as Acting President.

**Section 4**
Whenever the Vice President and a majority of either the principal officers of the executive departments or of such other body as Congress may by law provide, transmit to the President pro tempore of the Senate and the Speaker of the House of Representatives their written declaration that the President is unable to discharge the powers and duties of his office, the Vice President shall immediately assume the powers and duties of the office as Acting President.

Thereafter, when the President transmits to the President pro tempore of the Senate and the Speaker of the House of Representatives his written declaration that no inability exists, he shall resume the powers and duties of his office unless the Vice President and a majority of either the principal officers of the executive department or of such other body as Congress may by law provide, transmit within four days to the President pro tempore of the Senate and the Speaker of the House of Representatives their written declaration that the President is unable to discharge the powers and duties of his office. Thereupon Congress shall decide the issue, assembling within forty-eight hours for that purpose if not in session. If the Congress, within twenty-one days after receipt of the latter written declaration, or, if Congress is not in session, within twenty-one days after Congress is required to assemble, determines by two-thirds vote of both Houses that the President is unable to discharge the powers and duties of his office, the Vice President shall continue to discharge the same as Acting President; otherwise, the President shall resume the powers and duties of his office.

**Twenty-Sixth Amendment**
**Section 1**
The right of citizens of the United States, who are eighteen years of age or older, to vote shall not be denied or abridged by the United States or by any State on account of age.

**Section 2**
The Congress shall have power to enforce this article by appropriate legislation.

**Twenty-Seventh Amendment**
No law, varying the compensation for the services of the Senators and Representatives, shall take effect, until an election of Representatives shall have intervened.

# Author Biography

**Aubrey G. Stephens** is a retired teacher from Mississippi. He has Masters degrees in both theater and history, with certification in English, science, and special education. He is also a marine veteran and former military officer. The rumor that he has attempted to blow up the earth is just that, though he was on combat missile crew alert when the NORAD radar had a fail and reported that there were Soviet inbound missiles headed for the U.S. He is a trained martial artist with a second degree black belt in karate, brown belt in judo, and brown belt in Kendo. He also studied and taught European fencing for many years. His hobbies include recreating the Middle Ages and the American Civil War. He is squired to one of the S.C.A. (Society of Creative Anachronism)'s most well-known knights and at this time holds the rank of Captain in Co. A 24$^{th}$ Mississippi Cavalry. He has acted, written, directed, and done set design and construction for over 200 theatrical shows. Since his retirement, he has edited many books and become a professional writer. His collection, TALES OF THE INTERGALACTIC BARTENDERS GUILD, won a Pulp Factory Award. He enjoys swapping stories of the many sci-fi/fantasy conventions where he has worked, attended or been a guest.

www.ingramcontent.com/pod-product-compliance
Lightning Source LLC
Chambersburg PA
CBHW060522100426
42743CB00009B/1402

mouth. This is called belly-breathing. Repeat the actions of belly-breathing three times. Good. Now, do you feel different? Remember, when you are relaxed, you are strong.

**End of Excerpt from**
*DARKEST SECRETS OF PERSUASION AND SEDUCTION MASTERS: HOW TO PROTECT YOURSELF AND TURN THE POWER TO GOOD*
Copyright Tom Marcoux Media, LLC

**Purchase your copy of this book (paperback or ebook) at Amazon.com or BarnesandNoble.com**
See **Free Chapters** of Tom Marcoux's 23 books at http://amzn.to/ZiCTRj

# ABOUT THE AUTHOR

**Tom Marcoux** helps people like you fulfill big dreams. Known as America's Communication Coach and TFG Thought Leader, Tom has authored 23 books with sales in 15 countries. One of his *Darkest Secrets* books rose to #1 on Amazon.com Hot New Releases in Business Life (and in Business Communication). He guides clients and audiences (IBM, Sun Microsystems, etc.) to success in job interviewing, public speaking, media relations, and branding. A member of the National Speakers Association, he is a professional coach and guest expert on TV, radio, and print, and was dubbed "the Personal Branding Instructor" by the *San Francisco Examiner*.

Tom addressed National Association of Broadcasters' Conference six years running. With a degree in psychology, Tom is a guest lecturer at **Stanford University**, DeAnza, & California State University, and teaches public speaking, science fiction cinema/literature and comparative religion at Academy of Art University. Winner of a special award at the **Emmys**, Tom wrote, directed, and produced a feature film that the distributor took to the **Cannes film market**, and the film gained international distribution. He is engaged in book/film projects *Crystal Pegasus* (children's) and *TimePulse* (science fiction). See TomSuperCoach.com and Tom's well-received blog

at www.BeHeardandBeTrusted.com

Tom Marcoux can help you with **speech writing** and **coaching for your best performance.**
As Tom says, *Make Your Speech a Pleasant Beach.*
Join Tom's Linkedin.com group: *Executive Public Speaking and Communication Power.*

At Google+: join the community "Create Your Best Life – Charisma & Confidence"

Get a **Free** report: "9 Deadly Mistakes to Avoid for Your Next Speech and 9 Surefire Methods" at
http://tomsupercoach.com/freereport9Mistakes4Speech.html

Tom Marcoux has trained CEOs, small business owners, and graduate students to speak with impact and gain audiences' tremendous approval and cooperation. *Learn how to present and get thunderous applause!*

"Tom, Thanks for your coaching and work with me on revising my speech at a major university. Working with you has been so enlightening for me. Through your gentle prodding and guidance I was able to write a speech that connects with the audience. I wish everyone could experience the transformation I have undergone. You have helped me discover the warm and compelling stories that now make my speech reach hearts and uplift minds. This was truly an empowering experience. I cannot thank you enough for your great assistance." — J.S.

"Tom Marcoux has been an NAB Conference favorite [speaker] for six years. And he is very energetic."
– **John Marino,**
**Vice President, National Association of Broadcasters, Washington, D.C.**

"Using just one of Tom Marcoux's methods, I got more done in 2 weeks than in 6 months."
– **Jaclyn Freitas, M.A.**

**Become a fan of Tom's graphic novels/feature films:**
Fantasy Thriller: *Jack AngelSword*
type "JackAngelSword" at Facebook.com

Science fiction: *TimePulse*
www.facebook.com/timepulsegraphicnovel

Children's Fantasy: *Crystal Pegasus*
www.facebook.com/crystalpegasusandrose
See **Free Chapters** of Tom Marcoux's 23 books at http://amzn.to/ZiCTRj


**Special Offer Just for Readers of this Book:**

Contact Tom Marcoux at tomsupercoach@gmail.com for special discounts on books, coaching, workshops and presentations. Just mention your experience with this book.

www.ingramcontent.com/pod-product-compliance
Lightning Source LLC
Chambersburg PA
CBHW060522100426
42743CB00009B/1404